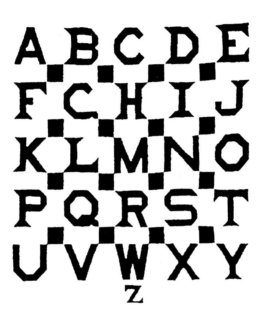

THE TEA PARTY

BY A SEVEN-YEAR-OLD GIRL

one day A gos for a walk she meet B look says A will you com to tea yes says
B Oh says A heres C caugt us up Halo C what time shal we com says C at 4 says
A says A oh Im going back Oh us to: hardly was she back the bell rung A went
to open the dor Ah Halo D how are you quit well says D look Im going to open
the windo Oh coohoo EFGHI can you com to tea yes let go J dont pull my
dress Oh halo J says A halo A says J but K says J your going to As tea yes Oh says
L heres J look J Ive bougt your bodis thanks says J oh says JMNOP are comming
look halo MNOP and heres QRSTU as well ding ding dingdong its 4 com on
says A oh choclet they sed look they take oh how late VWXYZ sit done

from CONTEMPORARY POETRY AND PROSE no. 2, Double Surrealist Number edited by Roger Roughton, June 1936

ALPHABETS
& OTHER
SIGNS

EDITED BY
JULIAN ROTHENSTEIN
AND MEL GOODING

THAMES AND HUDSON

THE EDITORS WOULD LIKE TO GIVE SPECIAL THANKS TO THE FOLLOWING PEOPLE WHO CONTRIBUTED
MATERIAL OR WERE GENEROUS IN OTHER WAYS :

Eric Ayers, David Batterham, Quentin Newark, Paul Elliman, Julia Farrer, Herbert Spencer, Alan Fletcher,
Lucy Virankabutra, Dennis Bailey, C E McNally, Clive Crook, Lee Ghai Kong, Ian Sturnfeldt, Natalie Barton,
Richard Adams, Nigel Coke, Amelia Gatacre, Matthew Tyson, Alastair Brotchie and Christabel Gurney

Designed by Julian Rothenstein

INTRODUCTION © Mel Gooding 1991
ARTS ET MÉTIERS GRAPHIQUES © Ruari McLean 1991
THE SPIRIT AND THE LETTER © Neil Crawford 1991

This edition © Redstone Press
This edition first published in Great Britain in 1993
by
Thames and Hudson Ltd, London

Printed and bound in China

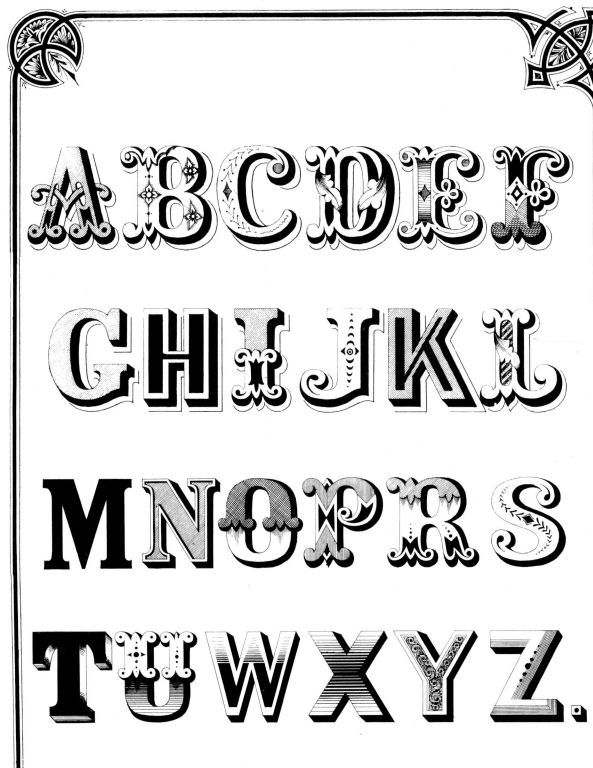

INDEX OF FEATURES

An introduction: MEL GOODING 9

Arts et Métiers Graphiques: RUARI McLEAN 27

French religious and political trademarks 47-49

Homage to American typefounders 54-63

Other alphabets 73-85

The Spirit and the Letter: NEIL CRAWFORD 94

Meccano alphabets and signs 102-104

Ampersands, indicators, fleurons
and other printers' clichés 107-115

Lettering by hand 124-131

Logos and trademarks 145-160

Wood types 162-171

Pages from *Arts et Métiers Graphiques:*
15, 21, 25, 26, 29, 35, 42, 50, 51, 67, 70, 91, 93, 98, 99, 100, 101, 134, 137, 141, 151,
159, 164, 166, 169, 179, 181

An Introduction

MEL GOODING

Of the making of alphabets there is no end. Letter forms and typefaces have been created in wonderful variety to serve a multitude of functions. Every job demands the right face, the lettering that will serve its purposes best, and many alphabets have been designed for particular tasks and specific media: the stonemason's lapidary, the stenciller's schematic, the needleworker's stitchable, as well as the manifold forms that are necessary to the printer's trade. Each has a character and a feel of its own, each bears the imprint of its time and the marks of its *milieu.*

Alphabets come in infinite diversity: in some the letter forms are simple, in others, complex and complicated, fantastic and extravagant. There are modest alphabets and flamboyant alphabets, silly alphabets and sad ones. Alphabets proliferate. In literate societies they are an index of human diversity: every child that learns to write invents its own, as distinctive as fingerprints.

Not all alphabets are equal. Some alphabets are highly legible, and others almost impossible to decipher, unintentionally funny or intentionally ludic. Some are consistently elegant, reflecting the grace and intelligence of their makers, fit for the transparent setting of subtle and beautiful language; some are workaday and simple, democratic in spirit, apt for plain writing; others are squat and ugly, betraying the brutality of their time and place in history; others are fanciful or idiosyncratic, drawing attention to their formal waywardness. In every case they are *expressive:* functional visual systems designed for communicative purposes, they nevertheless speak for themselves, assume style. They are visible artefacts of their culture, variously perfect, flawed, or just queer.

For many typographers and the printers and publishers they supply, especially those concerned with the setting of prose in books and newspapers, the perfect typeface is one in which the alphabet becomes invisible as the reader apprehends the matter carried by the complicated and rigorous arrangements of its individual characters. The set page is a clear window upon meaning, every letter-form balanced, and every relation between letters in words, and words in sentences, minimizing distraction from the message to the medium. 'Printing should be invisible' wrote Beatrice Warde, the writer and publicist for the Monotype Corporation in its golden years. For Stanley Morison, the doyen of typographers in that period, typography was 'the efficient means to an essentially utilitarian and only accidentally aesthetic end . . . Therefore, any disposition of printing material which, whatever the intention, has the effect of coming between author and reader is wrong.'

For such typographers, the revivalists of the great classical faces and the inventors of elegant new functional ones, like Morison himself, Gill and van Krimpen, the letter must modestly and discreetly serve the text ('If readers do not notice the consummate reticence and rare discipline of a new type it is probably a good letter,' wrote Morison). Clarity and legibility were the watchwords of these militant traditionalists, and in England they carried all before them in the great typographic revival of the years between the wars.

The task of the type-designer was to achieve a balanced face, in which each letter would aspire to tonal equality with every other, and to a non-assertive uniformity of effect. The printer's job was to set the page with a symmetrical balance, centering the text in such a way as to afford the least visual disturbance possible, and to ornament with taste and discretion only where the text allowed and the accepted aesthetic of the page required it.

These rigorous ideals, based upon principles of public service in a spirit disposed to the democratic dissemination of knowledge and ideas, were stolidly advocated in the writings of Morison, Gill, Paul Beaujon, Bruce Hegers and others. They were exemplified with grace in beautifully produced publications such as Francis Meynell's TYPOGRAPHY (1923), THE FLEURON (seven issues from 1923 to 1932), and Oliver Simon's SIGNATURE (first issue November 1935); and in a remarkable succession of printers' type-specimen books, notable among many others those issued by the Curwen Press (1928), Richard Clay & Sons (1930), and the Kynoch Press (1934). These latter contained alphabets set in every face used by the printer, in upper-case, lower-case, bold and italic, and in their various sizes, and frequently carried pages of text set and decorated to demonstrate the complete font available.

Splendid as they might be, these specimen books were essentially commercial in intention, and they were limited, of course, to those type alphabets that the printers actually stocked and used in book and magazine production. But it was always understood that the jobbing printer was necessarily at the heart of communication, the essential journeyman (the daily worker!) in the cause of radical reform. In the AMERICAN TYPEFOUNDERS MANUAL of 1941 some of the specimen pages were set with direct and eloquent statements of the democratic principles and functions of printing, while others contain wittily cryptic political messages. It should not surprise that one of the best typographical style books of the post-war days of hope was Michael Middleton's SOLDIERS OF LEAD, issued by the Labour Party in 1948, with an epigraph from Milton's AREOPAGITICA.

Whilst the revivalists, high-minded and idealistic, but fundamentally conservative, were determining the new directions of book, magazine and newspaper design in this country, elsewhere things were different. In Russia, Germany and Holland, a revolution in typography and layout was taking place, inspired by the utopian ideals of Modernism, and led not by letter designers and printers, but by major artists. In the pages of DE STIJL and Schwitters's MERZ, in the publications of the *Bauhaus,* in the work of Lissitzky, Moholy-Nagy, Bayer, Werkman, and many others, a new and aggressively asymmetric typography was adopted, and advocated for universal use. The sans serif types of *die neue typographie* were accorded the attributes of an honest and unornamented beauty and clarity.

The letter, freed from subordination to the word, leapt into visibility and proclaimed itself a concrete and independent component of the printed message. The setting of the message itself, poem or prose, advertisement or propaganda, aspired to the condition of the abstract image, entering the eye and the mind dynamically, challenging critical response, inviting reflection. 'There is a connection between modern typography and modern architecture' wrote Jan Tschichold, in his classic exposition ASYMMETRIC TYPOGRAPHY, 'but the new typography does not derive from the new architecture; rather both derive from the new painting, which has given to both a new significance of form . . . . [An abstract painting] is an instrument of spiritual power, a conception of harmony. . . . It is an appeal to order, a means for the improvement of mankind. It is not passive but dynamic'. The printed page was just such a mechanism, its energetic aesthetic having ethical purpose. The types and signs of this modernism will be more fully represented in Volume 2 of ALPHABETS AND OTHER SIGNS.

In France the stylish asymmetry and *chic* dispositions of letter and *motif* of the more advanced journals and magazines of the modern period derived, typically, from home-grown sources. They were appropriated with Gallic *insouciance* from the graphic wit and vigour of Toulouse-Lautrec, from the jazzy 'modernism' of *Art Déco,* first presented as such at the great Paris exhibition of 1925, from the elegant *mis-en-page* of the great *livres d'artistes,* and the poetic experiments of Mallarmé and Apollinaire. This eclectic stylism is especially celebrated in the present compilation, in the pages from ARTS ET MÉTIERS GRAPHIQUES, and in essays by Ruari McLean and Neil Crawford.

The letter is the point at which the structures of language meet the ground of the visible. It comes long after speech in the order of things; long after the sounds uttered by humankind at its beginnings had separated into words, and these had been organised into systems of meaning. It was preceded in the world by visual signs, and is now constantly accompanied by them. The sign, in its simple directness and its visibility, is the means by which the sounds of speech found their way towards the letter and the written word. In a book that presents the alphabet in many forms and many styles, and which is intended not only for practical use by designers, artists, poets and writers, but for anyone who loves letters in their infinite variety, it is proper for the sign to be a vigorous and enlivening presence.

This book is not like the many alphabet books and surveys that already exist, collections of particular kinds of alphabet; neither is it a type-specimen book, or a manual of style and layout. It is altogether more personal and idiosyncratic. It had its beginnings in the affections of its editors: for all manner of letterings and typographies; for the multifarious written and printed signs that jostle 'the visible word' and make their mark in the visual world; for fleurons and flourishes, decorations and clichés, vignettes, trademarks and logos. It has no programme. It is intended to be used; it is intended to delight.

JULY 1991

ABCDE

FGHIJK

LMNOPQ

RSTUV

WXYZ

ABCDEFGHIJKLMNOP
QRSTU · abc · VWXYZ
defghijklmnopqrstuvwxyz
12345 · COLLEGE · 67890
Adonis · Information · Orient

ABCDEFGHIJKLMNO
12 PQRSTUVWXYZ 67
345 abcdefghijklmn 890
ABEL · opqrstuvwxyz · MINE
Bretagne Combination Sardine

ABCDEFGHIJKLM
NOPQRSTUVWX
12345 · YZ · 67890
abcdefghijklmno
æ pqrstuvwxyz œ

LES VIGNETTES TYPOGRAPHIQUES DES GRAVEURS FONDEURS DE L'ÉPOQUE ROMANTIQUE

L'histoire des débuts de la vignette typographique française du XIXᵉ siècle est peu connue ; elle correspond à une crise très sérieuse du livre illustré français.

Avec la Révolution venait d'être close l'ère des fameuses éditions aux hors-texte en taille-douce, que Mariette, l'avisé connaisseur du XVIIIᵉ siècle, qualifiait de « gravure en petit », en préconisant le retour au bois gravé, essentiellement typographique.

Toutefois, même pendant la tourmente révolutionnaire, le livre de petit format à gravures sur métal en creux, reparaissait avec Prudhon, Fragonard jeune, Desenne, Copia, Royer, Queverdo, etc. Paul Didot l'aîné produisit alors quelques éditions illustrées, plus à la mode du jour, mais encore conçues selon l'ancienne tradition. Ainsi furent publiés quelques ouvrages fort appréciés : *Théatre de M. de Florian* (1791)

15

Ludlow 6-EC Gothic Extra Condensed

ABCDEF

GHIJKLM

NOPQRST

UVWX

NOTE

For the remainder of
this alphabet, points,
figures, other charac-
ters, information, etc.,
see the following page

Ludlow 6-EC Gothic Extra Condensed

ABCDEF

GHIJK

LMNOP

QRSTU

VWXYZ

ABCD
EFGHI
JKLMN
OPQRS
TUVW
XYZ

A B C D E F G H I J J K L M
N O P Q Q QU Qu R S T U V
W X Y Z Æ Œ Ç & É È Ê

A B C D E F G H I J J K L M N O P Q
QU R S T U V W X Y Z Æ Œ Ç É È Ê

1 2 3 4 5 6 7 8 9 0

a b c d e f ff fi ffi fl ffl g h i j k l
m n o p q r s t u v w x y z æ œ
ç é à è â ê î ô û ë ï ü . , : ; - ' ? !)

A A B B C C D D E E F G G
H I J J J K K L M M N N O
P P Q Q R R R S T T U V V W
X Y Z Æ Œ Ç & É È Ê

a b c d e f ff fi ffi fl ffl g h h i j k
k l m n o p q r s t u v v w w x y z
æ œ ç é à è â ê î ô û ë ï ü . , : ; - ' ? !)

Caractéristiques du Caslon Elzévir Romain et
Caslon Elzévir Italique, dans le corps 28.

ARTILLERIE
DE FRANCE,
CORPS ROYAL.

DE PAR LE ROI.

LES Jeunes Gens qui defirent entrer au Service de SaMajefté, ne peuvent choifir un Corps plus avantageux ; ils y trouveront des Maîtres de Mathématiques & de Diflein, entretenus par le Roi, & feront, fuivant leur goût, attachés aux Compagnies de Sapeurs, Canoniers, Bombardiers & Ouvriers. La Paie plus forte que dans aucune autre Troupe, augmente jufqu'à vingt-un fols par jour, fuivant l'ancienneté. Le Roi a créé dans chaque Régiment de ce Corps, vingt Places d'Officiers pour les Sujets les mieux inftruits dans la manœuvre de l'Artillerie. Tous les Emplois de Garde-Magafin, Capitaine de Charois, Officier de Canonier Garde-Côtes, Artificier & Salpétrier du Royaume font réfervés, par ordre de Sa Majefté, à ceux qui ont fervi dans ce Corps. Les Ouvriers, Charrons, Charpentiers, Serruriers, Forgeurs, y font employés de leur Métier, & payés fuivant leurs talents jufqu'à trente fols par jour. On n'y reçoit que des Gens connus, fachant lire & écrire, ou d'âge à l'apprendre.

Il faut s'adreffer, pour être reçu, à M. HEDOUIN, Capitaine audit Corps, rue de la groffe Clef.

A B C D E F G H I

J K L M N O P Q R

S T U V W X Y Z &

1 2 3 4 5 6 7 8 9

BRUSH LETTERS FOR MARKING PURPOSES—MODERN STYLE.

ABCDEFGHIJKLM NOPQRSTUVWX

YZ&... abcdefghijklmnopqrstuvwxyz

1234567890.

Enquire, Huntington, Chicago, Rochester,
Buffalo, Cleveland, Milwaukee, Ohio.

Hill Standard Book Co.,
No. 103 State St.,
Chicago, Ill's.

PLAIN ROMAN LETTERS.

A B C D E F G H I J K L

M N O P Q R S T U V W

X Y Z . & Æ Œ

a b c d e f g h i j k l m n o p q

r s t u v w x y z . æ œ 1 2 3 4 5

6 7 8 9 0 . $ £

ANTIQUE POINTED EXTENDED.

A B C D E F G H I J K
L M N O P Q R S T U V
W X Y Z & .
1 2 3 4 5 6 7 8 9 0 .

ONE-HAND DEAF AND DUMB ALPHABET.

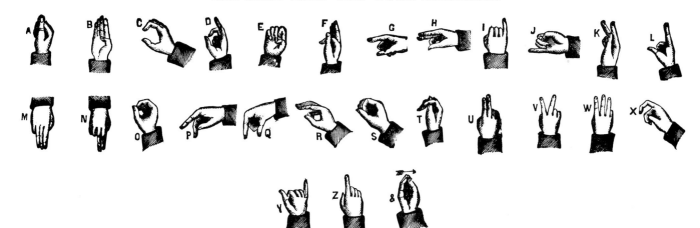

DORIC.

A B C D E F G H I J K L M N O P
Q R S T U V W X Y Z ?
a b c d e f g h i j k l m n o p q r s
t u v w x y z & $ 1 2 3 4 5 6 7 8 9 0 .

POINTED CONDENSED.

A B C D E F G H I J K L M N O P Q R S T
U V W X Y Z & $ 1 2 3 4 5 6 7 8 9 0 ? .

L'ARTISTE

PEINTRE DE LETTRES

Paris, MONROCQ FRERES Edit.rs
3 r Suger.

a b c d e f g h i j k l m

1 2 3 4 5 6 7 8 9 0

n o p q r s t u v x y z

TABLE DES RÉCITS DE LA CROISADE DES ENFANTS

récit du goliardar. page 3

récit du kalandar. p. 13

récit du pape innocent trois. p.

récit de françois longuejoue. p.

récit de trois petits enfants. p. 23

récit du pape grégoire neuf. p. 49

récit de la petite allys. page 43

récit du lépreux. page &

Qu'est-ce que la nouvelle typographie

QU'EST-CE QUE LA NOUVELLE TYPOGRAPHIE ET **Q**UE VEUT-ELLE **?**

O**N**

Arts et Métiers Graphiques

RUARI McLEAN

ARTS ET MÉTIERS GRAPHIQUES, that marvellous French magazine of the graphic arts, was the conception of Charles Peignot, who in 1923 took over the management of two French typefounding firms who had amalgamated, Deberny and Peignot. A & MG appeared every two months, from September 1927 until the last number, 68, in May 1939. It is, I think, the only periodical that covered all the graphic arts in France during the inter-war period and is certainly the most important source on French typography of that time. It was also highly entertaining and visually exciting.

Peignot and his friends, who included Jean Cocteau, Cassandre, Jean Carlu, Paul Colin, Charles Lupot and Maximilien Vox, formed a group known as U A M (Union des Artistes Modernes) who were, in Peignot's words, 'strongly against anything that was backward-looking'. Hence they did not think a lot of English typography or the output of the Monotype Corporation in London, which they saw as largely concerned with typographic revivals. No doubt for that reason, there is only one article over Stanley Morison's name in the entire 68 issues of A & MG, entitled NON-STOP (No 23, May 1931). This is Morison's account, translated into French, of his journey from London to Edinburgh on the footplate of the 'Flying Scotsman', accompanied by photographs of the magnificent locomotives of those days. (Significantly perhaps, Morison's name is mis-spelled.)

However, A & MG was far from being assertively avant-garde in its presentation. It followed the same format (308 x 245mm approx) for its whole life, and the same basic editorial plan. It had paper covers, contained not less than 80 pages, and was side-stapled, to accommodate a variety of papers and insets, often mounted on stiff paper or card. Sections were printed by different printers: for example, the pages of the first issue came from at least eight printers, including Mourlot, Draeger and Enschedé in Haarlem.

Every issue (except the occasional special numbers on Photography, Caricature, Publicity, etc.) began with a literary text (the first three were by Paul Valéry, Valéry Larbaud and André Suarez) printed on special paper as a demonstration of fine words set in fine typography — sometimes surprisingly traditional, sometimes highly imaginative in a typically French way, inspired by Vox; and never in the style of *die neue Typographie*. In later issues these texts were sometimes historical and included music.

Typography, lettering and type design, and the history of writing, were all dealt with fully on an international basis, but always in a French style. For example,

no. 19 (Sept. 1930), contains a well-illustrated 8-page article by Jan Tschichold: 'Qu'est-ce que la nouvelle typographie, et que veut-elle?' in which the article's heading, clearly not designed by Tschichold, is a wittily French version of *die neue Typographie* and shows a better understanding of what it was all about than was usual in Britain and the United States in the 1930s. The traditional niceties of type-setting and page design as observed in Britain by Morison, Meynell and Simon, or in Germany by Poeschel, were not the style of A & MG, although such careful work was quite often illustrated — and with admiration. French typography could be startlingly different — see, for example, Thibaudeau's MANUEL FRANÇAIS DE TYPOGRAPHIE MODERNE (1924) or Tolmer's MIS EN PAGE (1931). The French were much more interested in illustration, and this was a theme running through the entire life of A & MG.

Two other regular features of the magazine were sections entitled L'OEIL DU BIBLIOPHILE — for book collectors — and ACTUALITÉ GRAPHIQUE, showing posters and publicity. This was a great period of poster design in France: the work of Cassandre (who designed the Peignot and Bifur typefaces for Deberny & Peignot) appeared in nearly every issue, along with Colin, Carlu, Loupot, Bradovitch, Nathan and others. A & MG's cover for no 25 in Sept. 1931 was designed by Cassandre, using sans serif wood letters in large sizes, which, I believe, was noticed in England and echoed, a bit later, by Harling on the covers of his TYPOGRAPHY.

Painting, sculpture and architecture as such were not subjects for A & MG, but, for example, there were articles on exhibition design, and 'Les monotypes de Degas'. Drawing, etching and engraving, whether or not for books, were always given a lot of space, with superb reproductions in colour or from original plates.

Perhaps the most characteristic and endearing feature of A & MG was the richness and variety of its subsidiary articles. In one issue, for example, we find Flemish drawings, by Van der Goes, Bosch, Bruegel etc.; Romantic period greetings cards; and early woodcuts of skiing. In another, articles on the old paper mills of the Auvergne, Pear's Soap advertising in Britain, early Chinese colour printing, design and sculpture in cooking and pastry-making, Gerard de Nerval as printer, and modern travel publicity. That could be followed by articles on Man Ray, *trompe l'oeil,* the techniques of wall-paper manufacture, haberdashery labels, and constructions, chiefly for children, in paper. And in every issue, beautifully printed colour inserts and insets on special papers.

ARTS ET MÉTIERS GRAPHIQUES was, like Paris itself, infinitely varied, often absurd, and always fun.

ABCDEFG
HIJKLMN
OPQRSTU
VWXYZ&
abcdefghi
jklmnopq
rstuvwxyz
123456789

PU BLI CITÉ POUR DE LA FUMÉE

Pierre Louys, dans un de ses contes, parle d'une volupté nouvelle, inconnue des Anciens, celle que procure la consomption d'une cigarette. L'on peut dire qu'aujourd'hui fumer est devenu pour nous un véritable besoin superflu, et le tabac le plus populaire des produits de luxe. Il faut être juste, c'est une gageure que de vouloir proposer sous un aspect séduisant un menu cylindre régulier et uni de sept centimètres de long, dont la fonction est de s'évanouir en fumée dans l'espace de cinq minutes. Un tel objet de forme implacablement géométrique ne permet guère d'interprétations graphiques et par sa taille paraît minuscule dans la moindre composition. Quant aux variations sur la fumée et ses volutes, elles sont devenues d'une banalité telle qu'il vaut mieux n'en point parler. Restent donc pour présenter au public l'aliment quotidien de sa fumivore passion le développement et l'illustration des idées de volupté ou de rêve, de luxe ou d'élégance, de plaisir confortable. Idées élémentaires certes, mais suffisantes puisqu'elles peuvent aussi bien servir à vanter la qualité du produit employé et son arome, à désigner flatteusement son origine, à évoquer la joie du consommateur placé dans une ambiance choisie, à mettre en valeur « l'objet » lui-même — pipe, cigare ou cigarette — accompagné de ses accessoires ordinaires — cendriers, fume-cigarettes, etc.— qu'à signaler enfin un certain cachet de présentation et des prix, et qui, au surplus, sont particulièrement accessibles à toutes les clientèles féminines ou internationales puisque aussi bien, maintenant, la cigarette est devenue aussi universelle que la poudre de riz et le cinéma. Est-il utile de dire que chaque peuple, qu'il s'agisse d'emboitages, de pancartes, d'annonces ou d'affiches, apporte à la propagande de ses tabacs un tour d'esprit particulier, assez représentatif de sa personnalité. Les Allemands s'inspirent souvent de l'histoire et usent d'un certain expressionisme, les Américains et les Ang'ais se sont tournés vers l'humour et le « flirt », tandis que les Français, qui « ont du goût » comme chacun sait, préfèrent une certaine tournure décorative, la plupart du temps du plus mauvais goût, il faut bien l'avouer. Jetons donc un coup d'œil — rapide, car nous ne saurions tout examiner en détail dans un seul article — sur la façon dont nous sommes conviés (compositions attractives, ou anecdotes suggestives) à cette joie abstraite (bien que physique) et fugitive qui consiste à aspirer quelques bouffées d'une fumée savoureuse et odorante. D'abord un peu d'histoire et de géographie exotique. La maison Neuerburg a édité en 1927 et 1930 deux petits volumes de présentation heureuse donnant tous les détails qu'on peut désirer savoir sur la découverte du tabac, son introduction en Europe, sa culture et les préparations qu'il subit et sur tous les instruments dont il a nécessité la création pour sa consommation. L'un de ces deux opuscules s'orne d'un papier de garde romantique et charmant et contient les reproductions remarquables de pipes en terre, en bois et en porcelaine, de cure-pipe, de tabatières, de pots à tabac, de râpes, etc. de tous pays et du XVIIe siècle à nos jours, ainsi que de nombreuses caricatures et titres de musique. C'est là une réunion d'images qui, certes, n'épuise pas le sujet, mais offre malgré tout un intérêt certain. Au reste l'Allemagne est, malgré quelques fautes et erreurs de goût, le pays qui semble, avec quelques États d'Europe centrale, avoir fait le plus d'efforts réellement artistiques pour la présentation et la publicité de ses tabacs. Je sais bien que certaines marques comme *Hallali* représentant une chasse dans le goût des vieilles gravures sur bois, ou *Salvator*, représentant un moine, n'offrent guère de rapport avec l'idée de « pétun », mais qu'importe, ce sont des réussites que ces images tout comme celles hautes en couleurs représentant un *Éléphant* rouge, ou un *Tigre* jaune sur fond rose chassé par des Indiens fumeurs de calumet. La maison Ravenklau, pour gagner la bouche des dames, si j'ose m'exprimer ainsi, fait paraitre une série d'annonces, d'un style beaucoup classique nous montrant des automobilistes, des aviatrices, des cavalières, des baigneuses, des chasseresses, des skieuses, des yachtwomen, des Vénus de Sleeping, des promeneuses de luxe flanquées de trois magnifiques chiens, voire des tireuses à l'arc, modernes Walkyries, toutes plus fumeuses les unes que les autres, tandis qu'enfin la maison Neuerburg, fidèle au genre historique, sans doute parce que vieille maison, s'en tient à des visions traditionnelles des charmes du temps passé. Plus facilement aimable, plus publiquement publicitaire est le ton de l'Angleterre et celui de l'Amérique, sensibles aux chromos sentimentaux, à l'humour intraduisible des « nonsenses » et des petites poésies genre « nursery rimes » et toujours facilement convaincues par un « slogan » vigoureusement et elliptiquement persuasif. A ce titre les campagnes publicitaires des Chesterfield, des Abdullah, des Craven, des Lucky Strike sont remarquablement symptomatiques d'une certaine psychologie commerciale à défaut de véritables qualités artistiques. Heureux pays où l'on vit à l'ombre pratique des girls en fleurs de kodack, du Lyons tea, et de Palmolive. Aimez-vous les jeunes filles frai-

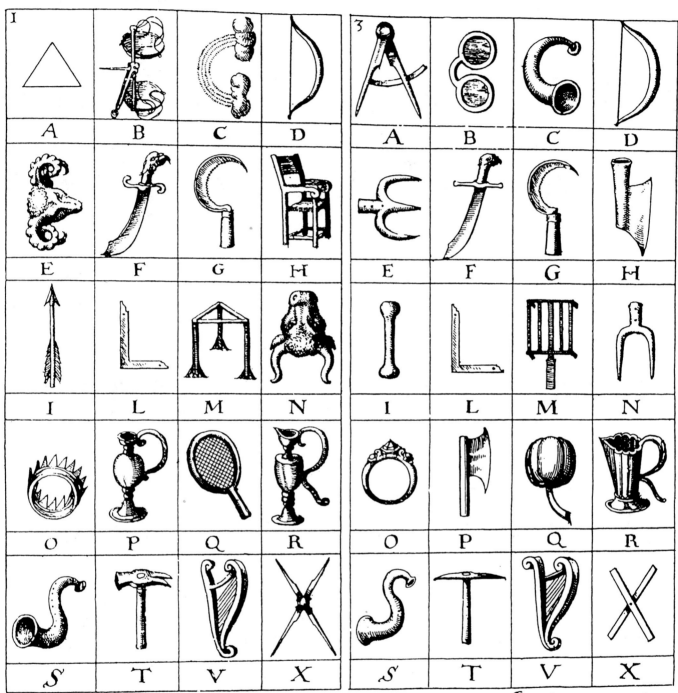

I				3			
A	B	C	D	A	B	C	D
E	F	G	H	E	F	G	H
I	L	M	N	I	L	M	N
O	P	Q	R	O	P	Q	R
S	T	V	X	S	T	V	X

Ordo Characterum Arithmetico-
rum in hac arte.

Characteres Arithmetici in
hac arte.

30

AAAABBBCCCDD

EFGHIIJKKKK

LMMMNNNOPPP

QQQRRSSTT

VVUWXXY

YYZŒabccdef

ghijkklmnopqrfst

vuwwxyyzæ&ffft

ABCCOEFGCHIJ
KLMNNOPORST
VVXYZ.ÆM

SACRED AND OTHER MONOGRAMS.

ABCDEFGHI
JKLMNOPQR
STUVWXYZ
1234567890
·REVOLUTION·
·WASHINGTON·

·CARACTÈRE DOUBLET· · SCHRIFTGIESSEREI CH. DOUBLET, PARIS.

ABCDEFGHIJ
KLMNOPQRS
TUVWXYZ
1234567890

aabcdefghijklm
nopqrstuvwxyz

A B C D E F G H I

J K L M N O P Q R

S T U V W X Y Z

a b c d e f g h i j k

l m n o p q r s t u

v w x y z

1 2 3 4 5 6 7 8 9 0

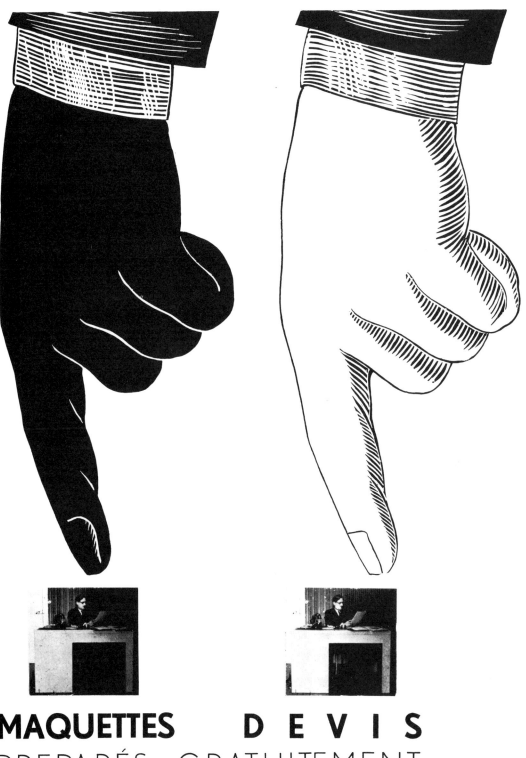

JUGEZ LA VALEUR DE NOS SERVICES PAR DEUX FAITS PRÉCIS

MAQUETTES **DEVIS**
PREPARÉS GRATUITEMENT

EDITIONS **PAUL·MARTIAL** PARIS

AFFICHES

CATALOGUES

DÉPLIANTS

abcdef

ghiklm

nopqrs

tuwxyz

ALPHABET OF THE FIFTEENTH CENTURY.

A B C D E F

G H I J K L

M N O P Q Q

R S T U V W

X Y Z

Alphabet cut in bone by French prisoners of war, Napoleonic Wars

BUFFON ALPHABET
DES
OISEAUX

WXYZ

ABCDE
FGHIJK
LMNOP
QRSTU
VWXYZ

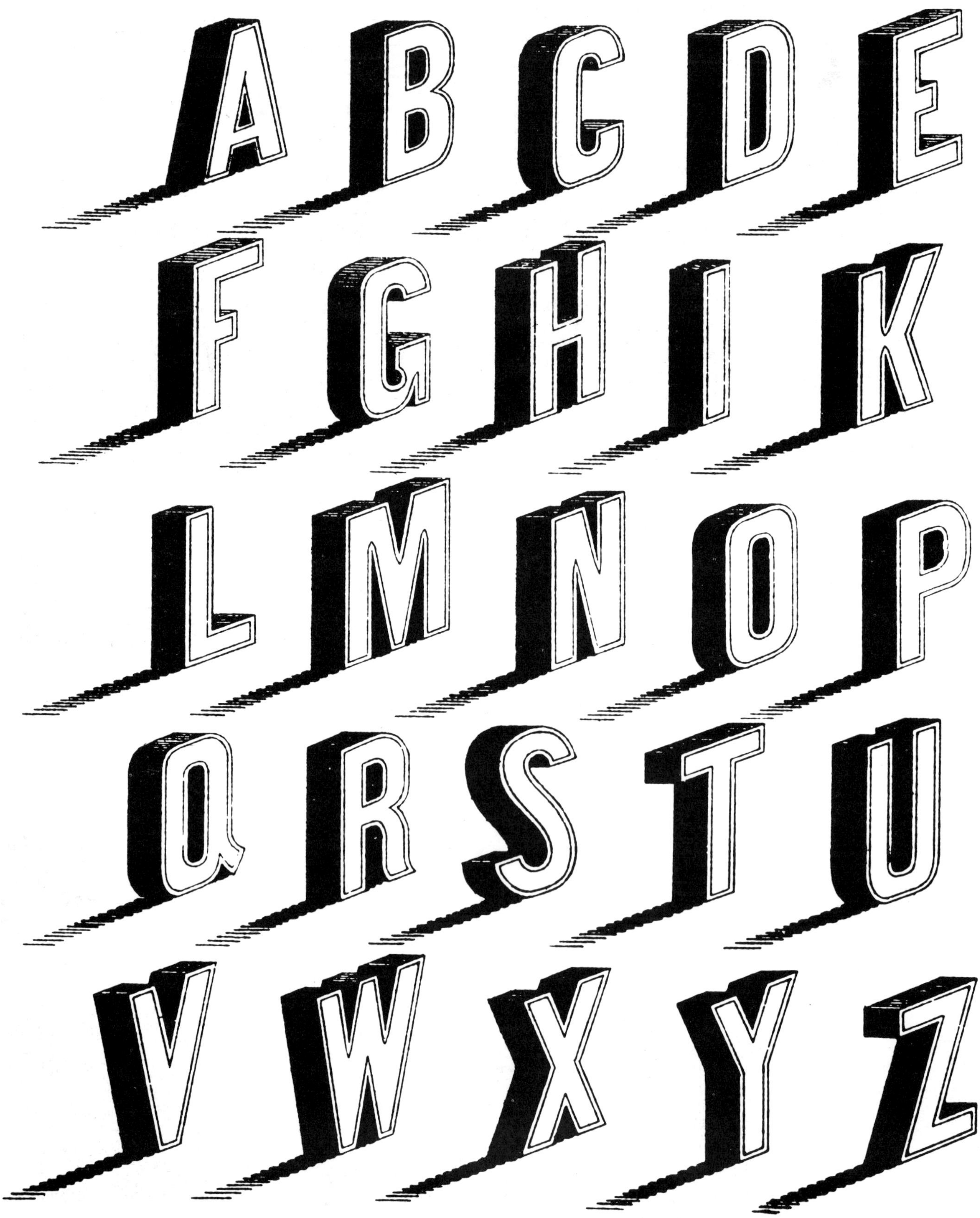

A B C D E
F G H I K
L M N O P
Q R S T U
V W X Y Z

INK SPOTS

B 12

PER FONT $1 25

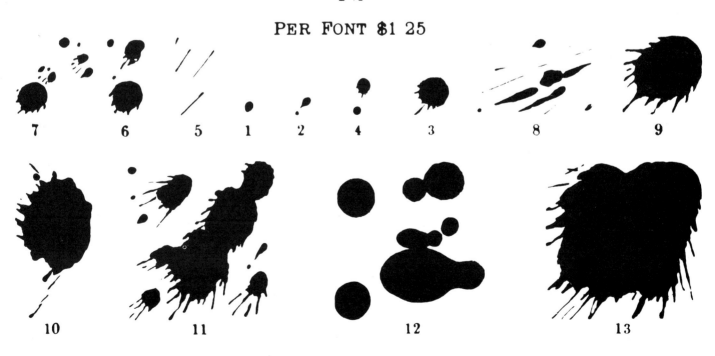

Lithographie d'André Derain.
(Les Quatre Chemins, Édit.).

ANDRÉ DERAIN

LITHOGRAPHE, XYLO-GRAPHE, AQUAFORTISTE

ANDRÉ DERAIN est venu à Paris en sabots. Du moins,

ABCDEFG
HIJKLMN
OPQRSTU
VWXYZ&!

abcdefghijklmn

opqrstuvwxyz

123456789

ABCDEFG
HIJKLMN
OPQRSTU
VWXYZ&!

abcdefghijklmn
opqrstuvwxyz!

123456789

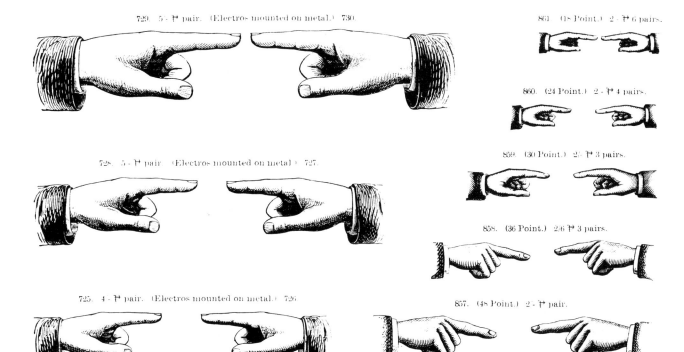

729. 5 - ℔ pair. (Electros mounted on metal.) 730.

861. (18 Point.) 2 - ℔ 6 pairs.

728. 5 - ℔ pair. (Electros mounted on metal.) 727.

860. (24 Point.) 2 - ℔ 4 pairs.

859. (30 Point.) 2/- ℔ 3 pairs.

858. (36 Point.) 2/6 ℔ 3 pairs.

725. 4 - ℔ pair. (Electros mounted on metal.) 726.

857. (48 Point.) 2 - ℔ pair.

Complete set of Shaded Indexes, assorted as above, 16 6: or omitting Nos. 729, 730, 14/-

ROBINSONS, BRISTOL.

B.200

ABCDEFGH
IJKLMNOP
QRSTUVXY
ZWÇÆŒ&

abcdefghij
klmnopqrs
tuvxyzwçæ
œ.,:;'-!?()„

1234567890

ABCDE
FGHIJKLM
NOPQRST
UVXYZWÇ
ÆŒ&

abcdefghij
klmnopqrs
tuvxyzwç
æœ.,:;'-!?()„

1234567890

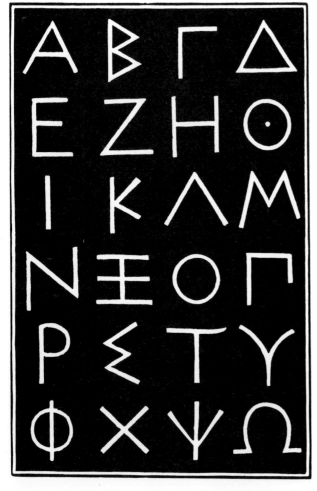

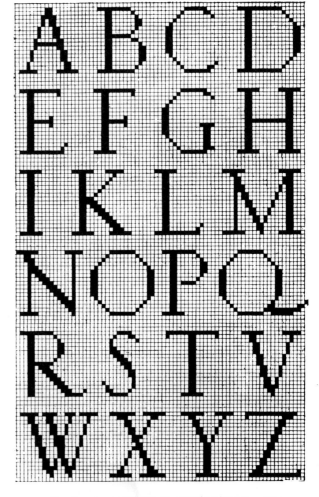

54. GREEK. FROM A STELE AT ATHENS. B.C. 394.

126. FROM THE LACE-BOOK OF GIOVANNI OSTAVS. 1590.

French trademarks with a religious or political slant, chosen by Louis
Barnier P.I.G., A.A. of the Collége de Pataphysiques from the files at
the French registry of trademarks, the Dépot des Marques in Paris.

LAXATIF
JEANNE D'ARC

PRÉPARÉ PAR

F. DELAS, Pharmacien de 1ʳᵉ Classe

de l'Ecole Supérieure de Paris

4, Rue de la République, ORLÉANS

Le *Laxatif Jeanne d'Arc* s'emploie contre les constipations et se prend à la dose de une ou deux cuillerées à dessert dans un demi-verre d'eau, le soir en se couchant.

PRIX : 1 fr. 25

LA JEANNE D'ARC

W C

Margarine

Moussant et roussissant à la poêle comme le vrai beurre

MARQUE DÉPOSÉE

VINAIGRERIE CENTRALE

12 MÉDAILLES-OR & ARGENT

FABᵠᵘᵉ DE   VINAIGRES

JEANNE D'ARC

ORLÉANS

DÉPOSÉ   **L. COURTOIS & FESSARD**   DÉPOSÉ

POIDS NET : 2.430.

CHANDELLE

PERFECTIONNÉE.

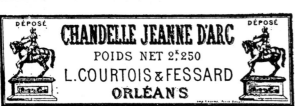

DÉPOSÉ   **CHANDELLE JEANNE D'ARC**   DÉPOSÉ

POIDS NET 2ᵏ,250

L. COURTOIS & FESSARD

ORLÉANS

PILULES
VITALES
JEANNE D'ARC
Régénératrices
du Sang

Guérissant l'Anémie, Maladies nerveuses, Chlorose, Paralysie, Rhumatisme, Ataxie locomotrice, Douleurs, Sciatiques, Maux de tête, Maladies des femmes, Suppression des règles, Pâles couleurs, Croissance rapide, etc., et, en général, toutes les maladies provenant d'un surmenage : Excès, épuisement prématuré, etc.

Mode d'emploi, consulter lo prospectus intérieur.

Prix : 1 Fr. 75 le Flacon

PHARMACIE JEANNE D'ARC
Fernand DELAS
Pharmacien de 1ʳᵉ classe
4, rue de la République, 4 — ORLÉANS

'Joan of Arc' brands

Anti-semitic champagne

Left wing bitters / Right wing bitters (same product)

L'Égyptienne est une des quatre grandes familles typographiques avec l'antique, le didot, l'elzévir • Dérivée de l'antique, ou caractère bâton, par un souci d'ornementation élémentaire elle se caractérise par des traits horizontaux terminant les jambages verticaux et en principe de même force que ceux-ci • L'Italienne, sous-famille de l'Egyptienne, se caractérise par un renforcement des empattements en hauteur et un amaigrissement des jambages • Une autre sous-famille est celle des maigrettes dont le type le plus connu est le caractère de machine à écrire • L'Egyptienne est une création du commencement du XIXᵉ siècle.

A N a n   A a   **A N a n**
B O b o   B b   **B O b o**
C P c p   C c   **C P c p**
D Q d q   D d   **D Q d q**
E R e r   E e   **E R e r**
            F f
            G g
            H h
            I i
            J j

ÉGYPT

F S f s   K k   **F S f s**
G T g t   L l   **G T g t**
H U h u   M m   **H U h u**
I V i v   N n   **I V i v**
J X j w   O o   **J X j w**
K Y k x   P p   **K Y k x**
L Z l y   Q q   **L Z l y**
M 6 m z   R r   **M 6 m z**
          S s
          T t
          U u
          V v
          X x
          Y y
          Z z

IENNE

ABCDEFGHIJKLMNOPQRSTUVWXYZ

abcdefghijklmnopqrstuvwxyz

ABCDEFGHIJKLMNOPQRSTUVWXYZ

abcdefghijklmnopqrstuvwxyz

ABCDEFGHIJKLMNOPQRSTUVWXYZ

abcdefghijklmnopqrstuvwxyz

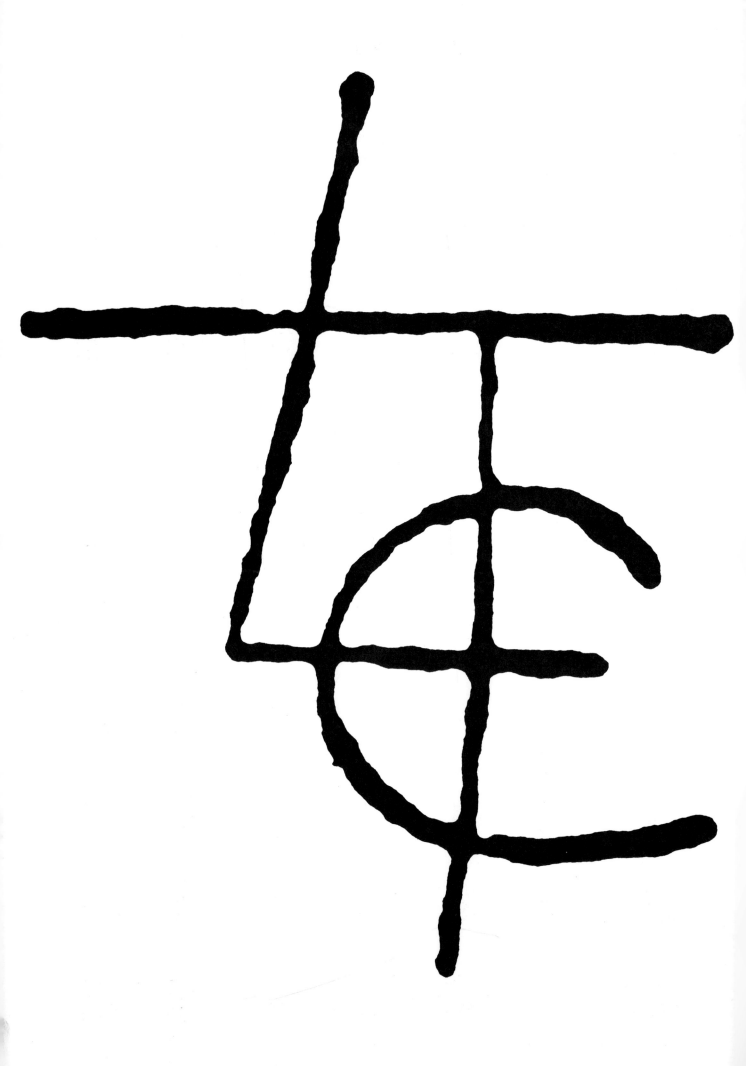

Monograms of artists and craftsmen

A B C D
E F G H I J K
L M N O P Q
R S T U V X
Y Z W Ç Æ
Œ &

a b c d e f g h i
j k l m n o p q r
s t u v x y z w
ç æ œ fi fl ff

.,:;'-!?()

1 2 3
4 5 6 7 8 9 0

Specimen pages from *The Book of American Types*, 1941

ABCDEFGHIJKL
MNOPQRSTUV
WXYZ&.,-':;.!?
$1234567890

144 Point   3 A

FURNITURE SALE

120 Point   3 A

BIG RUG

96 Point   3 A

NEW IRON

84 Point   4 A

FINE HOUSE

72 Point   5 A

LARGE ROOM

Characters in Complete Font

ABCDEFGHIJKL
MNOPQRSTUV
WXYZ&.,-':.¡!?

Fonted and sold separately:

$1234567890

Figures—72 to 144 point

AKMNS

Grotesque Characters—72 to 144 point

60 Point 4 A

DINE

96 Point 3 A

MEN

48 Point 4 A

HAND SOME

84 Point 3 A

RIME

42 Point 5 A

PRUNE CORES

72 Point 3 A

HARK

36 Point 6 A

MAIDEN REMIND

30 Point 8 A

PRINTING GIGANTIC

24 Point 10 A

NEIGHBORS DISTRIBUTE

CHARACTERS IN COMPLETE FONT

A B C D E F G
H I J K L M N
O P Q R S T U
V W X Y Z & $
1 2 3 4 5 6 7
8 9 0 . , - ' ' : ; ! ?

For a matching face in smaller sizes see Bank Gothic Condensed Medium on Page 155

120 Point 3 A

DESIRING

96 Point 3 A

SPECIMENS

Announcing another meeting of the **REGAL SOCIAL CLUB**, on Wednesday Evening, in the Gold Room of Hotel

JULY 3rd

CHARACTERS IN COMPLETE FONT

AABCDEFG
HIJKLMNO
PQRSTUVW
XYZ&$123
4567890¢
.,-'':;!?

84 Point 3 A

BURNISHED

72 Point 4 A

FINE DESIGNS

60 Point 5 A

MODERN HOUSE

48 Point 5 A

ATTRACTIVE SALES

120 Point 3 A

CARDS WON

96 Point 3 A

RACKET PROBE

84 Point 3 A

EXCITING GAMES

72 Point 3 A

BOY FOUND MONEY

60 Point 4 A

BIG FIRE

48 Point 6 A

NEW KING

42 Point 7 A

HEADLINES

Characters in Complete Font

ABCDEFG
HIJKLMN
OPQRST
UVWXYZ
&$1234
567890
.,-'':;!?

36 Point 8 A

HURRICANES

30 Point 8 A

LOVELY SPRING
COMING NORTH

24 Point 12 A

SIGNING MEASURE
FIGHTS CHAMPION

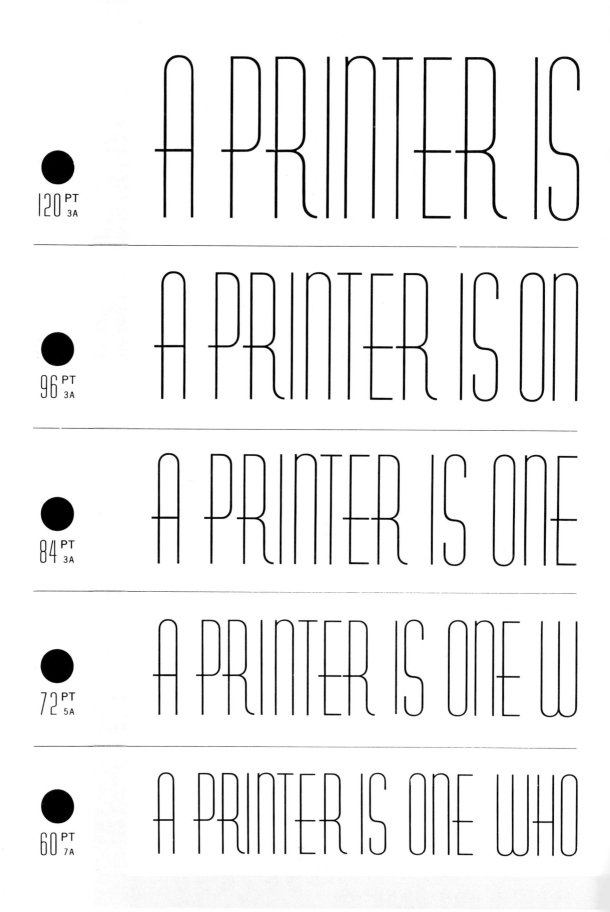

120 PT 3A — A PRINTER IS

96 PT 3A — A PRINTER IS ON

84 PT 3A — A PRINTER IS ONE

72 PT 5A — A PRINTER IS ONE W

60 PT 7A — A PRINTER IS ONE WHO

AABCDEFGHIJKKLMMNNOPQRSTU

A PRINTER IS ONE WHO SETS TRUTHS ON END AND STAMP

48 PT
9A

A PRINTER IS ONE WHO SETS TRUTHS ON END AND STAMPS THEM WITH A

36 PT
11A

A PRINTER IS ONE WHO SETS TRUTHS ON END AND STAMPS THEM WITH A MIGHTY

30 PT
14A

A PRINTER IS ONE WHO SETS TRUTHS ON END AND STAMPS THEM WITH A MIGHTY IMPRESSION UPON

24 PT
20A

A PRINTER IS ONE WHO SETS TRUTHS ON END AND STAMPS THEM WITH A MIGHTY IMPRESSION UPON THE CONSCIOUS

18 PT
25A

VWWXYYZ&.,-`´:;!?+$1234567890

Giving vi

Giving voit

Giving voice

Giving voice ti

Giving voice to th

Giving voice to the co

Giving voice to the count

GIVING VOICE TO THE CO
giving voice to the countless

GIVING VOICE TO THE COUNTL
giving voice to the countless thousa

GIVING VOICE TO THE COUNTLESS THOU
giving voice to the countless thousands who tell their story in the printed word is the function of

GIVING VOICE TO THEI
giving voice to the countl ess thousands who tell the ir story in the printed word is the function of type. To

GIVING VOICE TO THE COUNTLESS THOUS
giving voice to the countless thousands who t ell their story in the printed word is the funct

GIVING VOICE TO THE COUNTLESS THOUSANDS WH
giving voice to the countless thousands who tell their story in the printed word is the function of type. To modulate

GIVING VOICE TO THE COUNTL
giving voice to the countless thou sands who tell their story in the pr inted word is the function of type. To modulate that voice is the func

GIVING VOICE TO THE COUNTLESS
giving voice to the countless thousands who tell their story in the printed word is the function of type. To modulate th at voice is the function of type design.

SPARTAN MEDIUM

ABCDEFG
HIJKLMN
OPQRST
UVWXYZ

abcdefghij
klmnopqrst
uvwxyzæœ

Dusk to Dawn in the life of a Man-about-town, as shown by twenty-six different scenes, each decorating a letter of this tippler alphabet.

A B C D E F G H I

J K L M N O P Q R

S T U V W X Y Z &

a b c d e f g h i j k l m

n o p q r s t u v w x y z

1 2 3 4 5 6 7 8 9

ABCDEFGHI
JKLMNOPQR
STUVWXYZ

1234567890

PUIS DIEU DIT•
«QUE LES EAUX
SE RASSEMBLENT
EN UN   SEUL LIEU• ET QUE LE SEC
PARAISSE•   IL APPELA
TERRE LE   SEC ET MER
L'ÉTENDUE   DES EAUX••
CE•FUT•LE   SECOND•JOUR

PUIS DIEU DIT •« QUE LA TERRE
SE COUVRE DE
VERDURE »
ET CELA FUT AINSI
••••DIEU FIT LES ARBRES

FANFOLD

A A B B C C D D E F F G G
H H I I J J K L L M M N N
O O P P Q Q R R S S T T U U
V V W W X X Y Y Z Z I I 2 2
3 3 4 4 5 5 6 6 7 7 8 8 9 9
0 0 $ $? ? ! ! & & 'S 'S

BULLETIN OFFICIEL
DES
MAITRES
IMPRIMEURS
—

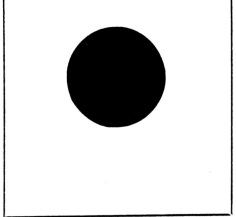

SUPPLÉMENT
AU
NUMÉRO DE
DÉCEMBRE 1929
—

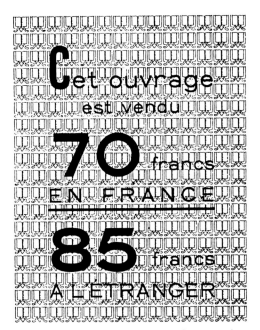

Cet ouvrage
est vendu
70 francs
EN FRANCE
85 francs
A L'ÉTRANGER

7, rue Suger
PARIS-VIe

Compte Chèque Postal 288-44

Couleurs de Cʜ. LORILLEUX et Cⁱᵉ.

Maquette d'Hᴇᴄᴛᴏʀ LAVA, à Lille.

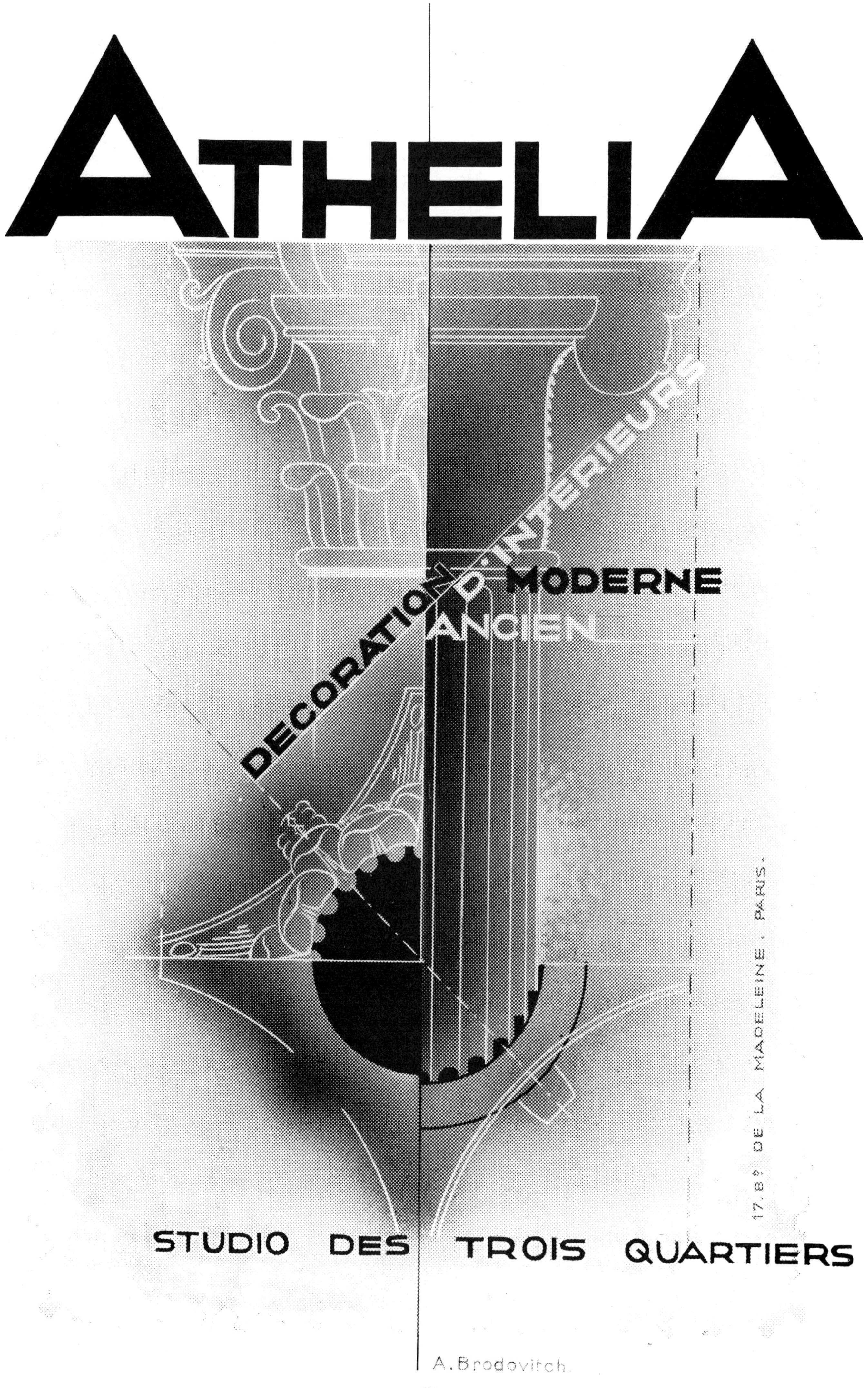

ATHELIA

DECORATION D'INTERIEURS
MODERNE
ANCIEN

17, 8° DE LA MADELEINE, PARIS.

STUDIO DES TROIS QUARTIERS

A. Brodovitch.

VWMNK

OCSQGA

XYZIEFL

UDBRP

JTH;,!?:

ABCDEFGHIJKLM

abcdefghijklmnopqrstuvwxyz.

NOPQRSTUVWXYZ.&c.

1234567890.

203. BRUSHWORK. QUASI-JAPANESE. L.F.D.

202. SQUARE-CUT. QUASI-CHINESE. L.F.D.

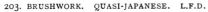

61. IRISH MS. FROM THE   BOOK OF KELLS. 8TH CENTURY.

АБВГД
ЕЖЗИКЛМ
НОПРСТ
УФХЦЧШ
ЩЪЬЮЯ

А Б В Г Д Е

Ж З И К Л М

Н О П Р С Т

У Ф Х Ц Ч Щ

Ъ Ы З Ю Я

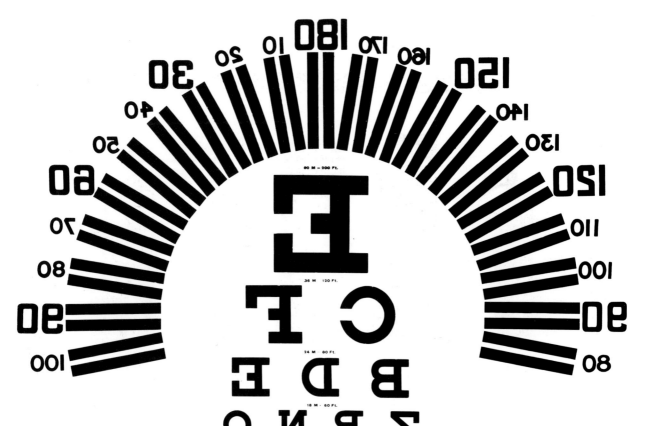

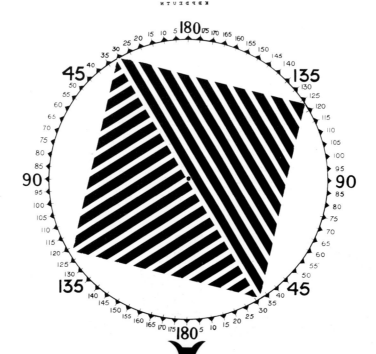

Optician's chart, 1930s

АБВГД
ЕХЗИЙ
КЛМНО
ПРСТУ
ФХЦЧШ
ЩЫЬЭЮЯ

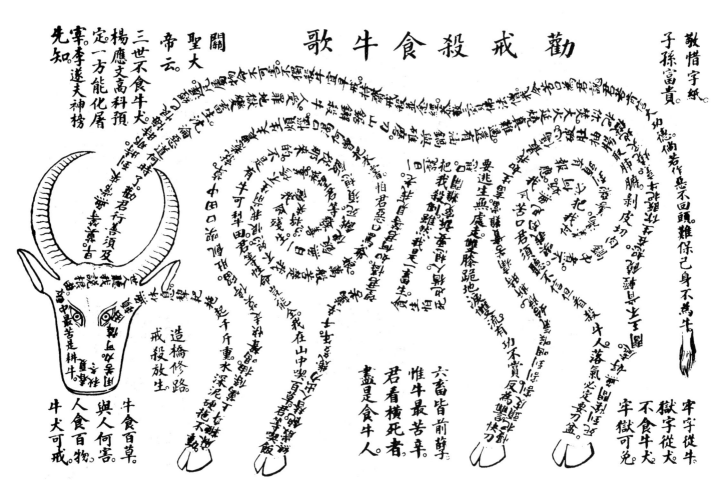

Chinese calligram of wild buffalo

Good Luck banner, South China

潮　愛　福
老　東　民
永　何　明
世　佛　陽

Chinese characters cut from wood

Cleverly stimulates the intricate, tangled appearance of Chinese writing. These letters would be picturesque for headline or initial use in suggesting Far Eastern atmosphere.

Systematische

LETTERGIETERIJ JOH. ENSCHEDÉ & ZONEN

Ornamenten

Serie 35

te Haarlem

3039   3040   3041   3042

3048   3047   3012   3051   3052

3053   3054   3055   3056

3057   3058   3059   3032   3033

3063   3064   3065   3066   3067   3068

THE MADRAS TYPE FOUNDRY,   -   -   MADRAS-1

அரிச்சுவடிகளும் குறிகளும்

தமிழ் மொழி						
அ	ஆ	இ	ஈ	உ	ஊ	எ
க	கா	கி	கீ	கு	கூ	கெ
ங	ஙா	ஙி	ஙீ	ஙு	ஙூ	ஙெ
ச	சா	சி	சீ	சு	சூ	செ
ஞ	ஞா	ஞி	ஞீ	ஞு	ஞூ	ஞெ
ட	டா	டி	டீ	டு	டூ	டெ
ண	ணா	ணி	ணீ	ணு	ணூ	ணெ
த	தா	தி	தீ	து	தூ	தெ
ந	நா	நி	நீ	நு	நூ	நெ
ப	பா	பி	பீ	பு	பூ	பெ
ம	மா	மி	மீ	மு	மூ	மெ
ய	யா	யி	யீ	யு	யூ	யெ
ர	ரா	ரி	ரீ	ரு	ரூ	ரெ
ல	லா	லி	லீ	லு	லூ	லெ
வ	வா	வி	வீ	வு	வூ	வெ
ழ	ழா	ழி	ழீ	ழு	ழூ	ழெ
ள	ளா	ளி	ளீ	ளு	ளூ	ளெ
ற	றா	றி	றீ	று	றூ	றெ
ன	னா	னி	னீ	னு	னூ	னெ

எழுத்துக்கள்					
ஏ	ஐ	ஒ	ஓ	ஔ	ஃ
கே	கை	கொ	கோ	கௌ	க்
ஙே	ஙை	ஙொ	ஙோ	ஙௌ	ங்
சே	சை	சொ	சோ	சௌ	ச்
ஞே	ஞை	ஞொ	ஞோ	ஞௌ	ஞ்
டே	டை	டொ	டோ	டௌ	ட்
ணே	ணை	ணொ	ணோ	ணௌ	ண்
தே	தை	தொ	தோ	தௌ	த்
நே	நை	நொ	நோ	நௌ	ந்
பே	பை	பொ	போ	பௌ	ப்
மே	மை	மொ	மோ	மௌ	ம்
யே	யை	யொ	யோ	யௌ	ய்
ரே	ரை	ரொ	ரோ	ரௌ	ர்
லே	லை	லொ	லோ	லௌ	ல்
வே	வை	வொ	வோ	வௌ	வ்
ழே	ழை	ழொ	ழோ	ழௌ	ழ்
ளே	ளை	ளொ	ளோ	ளௌ	ள்
றே	றை	றொ	றோ	றௌ	ற்
னே	னை	னொ	னோ	னௌ	ன்

Complete Tamil alphabet

Devils' signatures from 'the pact of the Demons with Urbain Grandier', 1634

ก ข ค ฅ ฆ ง จ ฉ

ช ซ ฌ ญ ฎ ฏ ฐ

ฑ ฒ ณ ด ต ถ ท ธ น บ

ป ผ ฝ พ ฟ ภ

ม ย ร ล ว ศ

ษ ส ห ฬ อ ฮ

ฯ ะ ั า ำ ิ ี ึ ื ุ ู เ แ โ ใ ไ ๆ

Complete Thai alphabet

85

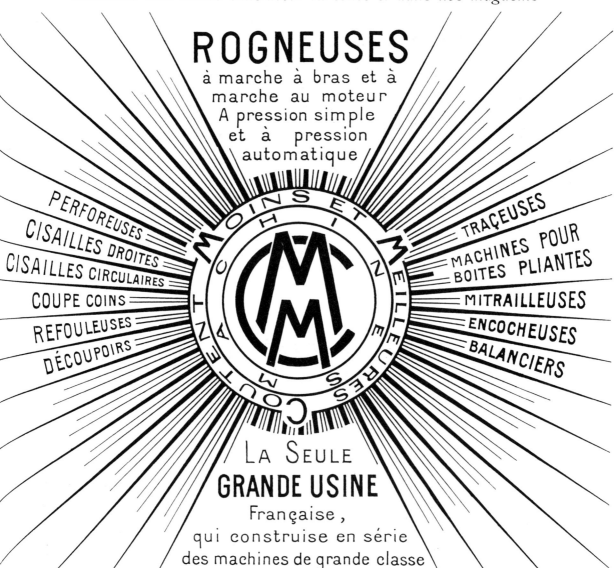
Le premier congrès patronal eut lieu à Tours, en 1848.

AGENCY GOTHIC

ABCDEFGHI
JKLMNOPQR
STUVWXYZ

1234567890
&.:;-`'!?$¢

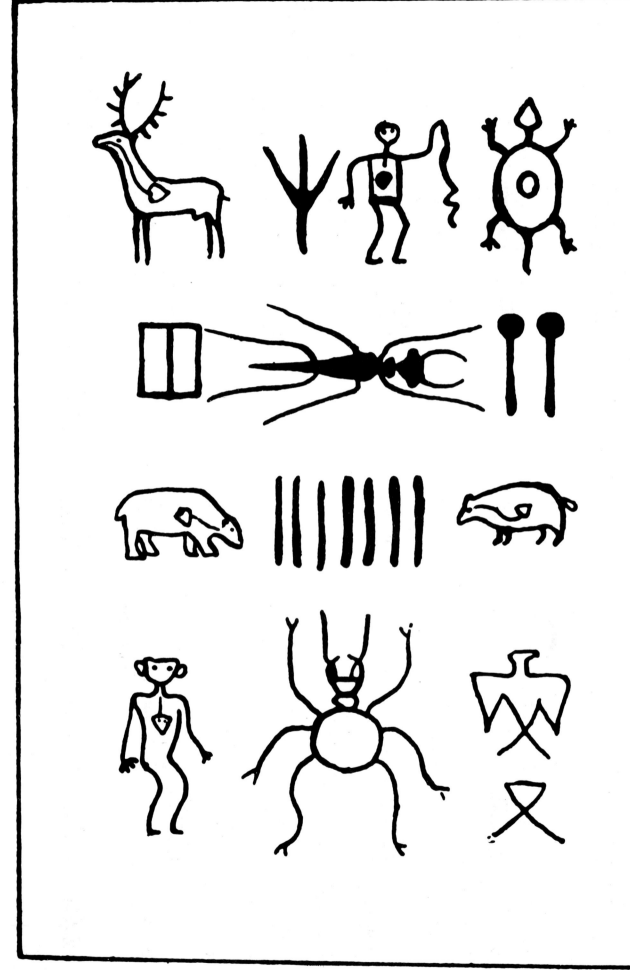

Signs incised in stone, prehistoric, Minnesota

88

A B C D E F
G H I J K L M
N O P Q R S T
U V W X Y Z

a b c d e f g h
i j k l m n o p q
r s t u v w x y z

1 2 3 4 5 6 7
8 9 0 ? & ¢
! . , — ( ) ' ; : $

ĀBCDEFGHI
JKLMNŌPQ
RSTŪVWXY
ZI1234
567890

LA GUERRE DE TROIE N'AURA PAS LIEU

pièce en deux actes par

Jean Giraudoux

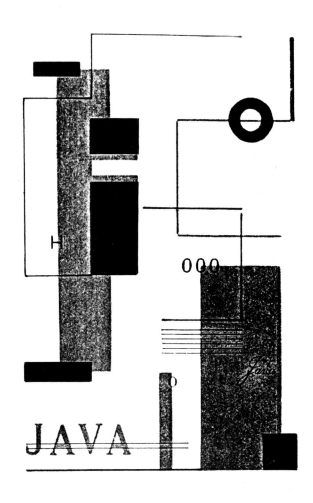

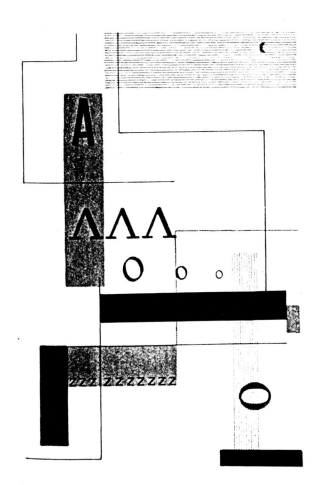

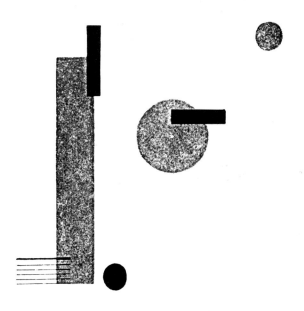

U kaple písková socha
ta korunovaná vrabčím hnízdem
pamatuje řadu lásek

Večer jdou milenci k lesu
a za nimi v patách se líbají modré stíny

11

The Spirit and the Letter: Poetry and Print

NEIL CRAWFORD

THE POET IS CONCERNED with the spirit; the printer with the letter. Together, they create an entity in which form and substance are not easily separated, yet the quality of the form — good or bad typography — does not directly affect the quality of the substance — the poet's word. The intellectual perception, emotional force and spiritual insight which finds its symbolism in a Shakespeare sonnet cannot be marred by a poorly cut typeface, nor can it be improved by superior press-work. As Aldous Huxley noted: *'Good printing cannot make a bad book good. But good printing can create a valuable spiritual state in the reader, bad printing a certain spiritual discomfort. The inwardness of letters is the inwardness of any piece of visual art regarded simply as a thing of beauty . . . At the same time our minds are sensitised by the contemplation of the simple visual beauty of the letters: they are made more susceptible of receiving the other and more complex beauties, all the intellectual and spiritual content, of the verse.'*

The classical tradition in the typographic treatment of a text is reflected in our habitual acceptance of standardised symmetrical formats and lack of compositional eccentricity. Typefaces have been refined to provide optimum legibility. The typographic forms of individual characters are rendered meaningless in themselves; the reader disregards the visual content of the letter-forms, for they combine to become merely phonetic signifiers of the signified concepts which together make up the meaning of the text. Thus traditional book typography can be considered as non-interpretive and non-expressive; the visual text is discreet, typography almost invisible; the letter serves the function of reading and nothing more.

This tradition of neutrality was challenged in the late 19th and early 20th century by poets and artists. They called into question not only the non-interpretive use of typography but also the historic division between the word and image. This led to explorations of new approaches to the structuring of a visible language, and a radical rejection of classical design.

Victorian and Art Nouveau typographies had, of course, developed their own distinctive aesthetic and visual habits, which had departed from classical decorum and simplicity, and which often drew attention to themselves in undesirable ways, inhibiting legibility without increasing the visual effect of the text. This had led to the Anglo-American 'Typographic Revival', led by Stanley Morison, Bruce Rogers and others, which sought to revive the order and dignity of late Renaissance printing. *'The first requisite in all book design is orderliness'* wrote Rogers. That these influential arbiters of taste had their own priority for typography is suggested, perhaps unconsciously, in his observation: *'Blank verse and poetry are the most difficult of all texts to arrange pleasingly, on account of the odd lengths of line and division into stanzas, which frequently need much juggling in the make-up to avoid awkward divisions.'*

Beatrice Warde (also known as the type critic Paul Beaujon), writing in 1936, was more practical: *'The poet himself will have helped to counteract the habits of the eye set up by prose-writers, whose art it is to carry the reader straight forward. The verses will have been "paused" by white space even in the manuscript. But the poet cannot always follow his work into the composing room and suggest that leading be put between lines, and more than the normal space between words, as further ways of slowing down the reader.'*

Tradition may have dictated the visual forms of verse to which the reader had become accustomed, with ordered lines of text, evenly leaded, all of one face and point size, but a liberation from conventional style and syntax demanded a liberation of typography as well. While the visual aspects of conventional verse are determined by metrical and stanza forms, open field poetry required the invention of new forms. In these, word spacing, lack of punctuation, and the expressive positioning of textual elements on the page take on the function of a rhythmic sound notation. The visible typographic structure becomes integral to the poem's dynamic structure; separate themes evolve into textual constellations, and graphic space becomes a dimension of content.

For the first major consideration of the printed text in space one must turn to Stephane Mallarmé. Attentive to both the typographic invention and variety of the daily press and advertising posters, he contrasted the dynamic *journal* to the predictable *livre*. For the poet the printing style of the newspaper, with its variety of headlines, sub-heads, features and advertisements, asserted a positive influence on his vision of what the 'book could be': *'A newspaper remains the starting point; literature empties itself into it according to our desire.'* For Mallarmé *'everything which the printing-house discovered is summed up at this point, under the name of* Press, *in an elementary form in the newspaper.'* Especially, the nature of newspaper production indicated how a writer might be involved *up to the last moment* — *'immediate or closely prior to the final proofing'* — in the physical casting of the text, successive proofs reproducing creative improvisation.

Mallarmé was one of the first to understand that the medium is part of the message. Without trying to provide a formula for what a book might be, he is impatient of the traditional typographic setting of verse, entailing *'the ceaseless successive coming and going of the glance . . . ending each line only to begin again at the following'.* Such agitation to the attention destroys the true delight of poetry which is to escape from the circumstances of the moment. *'Why should not a great fountain of thought or emotion, its phrases leading on in large type, one line a page, each modulated appropriately, hold the reader's attention throughout the duration of the book, appealing to his generous impulse to respond; whilst around it play a sprinkling of secondary flourishes, fragments of explanation, derivations?'*

All this led inevitably to UN COUP DE DÉS, Mallarmé's masterwork, a poem in which an essential constituent is its visual form. As Stefan Themerson remarked, UN COUP DE DÉS *'is arranged with a composer's rather than a compositor's logic'.*

Mallarmé revolutionised the concept of poetic structure, and initiated a revolution in typography carried through not by typographers but by artists, painter-poets, architects and designers working with the medium not as an end in itself but as a potentially vibrant means of communicating new ideas in a new way. Typefaces may have proliferated in the early years of the century, but after Mallarmé layout remained tied to the structures of conventional book typography until the advent of the Futurists.

The Futurists were adamant that form should intensify content. Marinetti wrote in 1909: *'The book will be the Futurist expression of our Futurist consciousness. I am against what is known as the harmony of a setting. When necessary we shall use three or four colours to a page and twenty different typefaces. We shall represent* hasty perceptions *in italic and express a* scream *in* bold type *. . . a new painterly typographic representation will be born on the printed page.'* In LES MOTS EN LIBERTÉ FUTURISTE (1919) he went further: *'free expressive orthography and typography'* would supposedly *'express the facial expressions and gestures of the reciter'!* Certainly LES MOTS EN LIBERTÉ used typography positively and expressively as a dynamic means to communication. The letter is no longer a conventional mute sign, but has become a material representation.

In fact the Futurists' choice of typefaces was intuitive; their innovation lay in flouting linear traditions and combining various type styles and weights to produce what is in effect a visual sound collage. Old typefaces may

From a typographic setting of Mallarmé's *Un Coup de Dés* (Neil Crawford 1988)

have been used, but they were revitalised by being freed from the straitjacket of horizontal use and employed as a flexible compositional element. The margin of the page was no longer the limit of form. Marinetti's break with typographic tradition was so complete that its repercussions can still be felt.

As early as 1910 Marinetti's FIGARO manifesto was in circulation in Russia. The majority of poets featured in the spate of Russian Futurist books produced around 1912 had actually trained as artists; when a poet is also an artist then innovation in textual form, in the *visual* presentation of the words, is likely to occur. The poetic contribution of the Russian Futurists was originally given graphic form through the medium of handlettering, but it was David and Vladimir Burlyuk's design contribution to Vassily Kamensky's poetry in TANGO SKOROVAMI (TANGO WITH COWS), and the textual treatment of Mayakovsky's play VLADIMIR MAYAKOVSKY — A TRAGEDY (1914), that were to have lasting and influential effects. In these the typography attempts to mirror the visual content of a text which is itself a form of painting with words, distributing the words, freed from normal syntactical constraints, over the whole page.

Considering that Mayakovsky's early work concerned itself with the interplay of verbal and visual elements, it is not surprising that David Burlyuk's anthology TREBNIK TROIKH (SERVICE BOOK OF THE THREE) published in 1913, contains Mayakovsky's tribute to primitive commercial art, the poem TO SHOP SIGNS. (*'Time turns advertisements into poems,'* wrote Stefan Themerson in 1951, *'and Time turns poems into advertisements, because Time changes the reader, and it depends on the reader whether a thing is or is not art.'*)

It was just after the 1917 revolution that Mayakovsky wrote: *'Revolution in content is unthinkable without revolution in form'* — the content was to be socialist and the form Futurist. By 1923 the form had become constructivist and content communist. El Lissitzky's design for his collection of poems DLYA GOLOSA (FOR READING ALOUD), published that year, was to make it a milestone in typographic history. Lissitzky's approach was innovatory in that he designed an expressive title page for each poem together with a symbolic thumb index to the contents. Although parts of the text were set in a conventional manner, his two-colour treatment of each poem's opening achieves a remarkable dynamic visuality using only readily-available type fonts and case furniture, whose restrictions (of which he was only too aware) he transcended triumphantly. Lissitzky said of the book: *'Just as the poet unites concept and sound, I have tried to create an equivalent unity using the poem and typography.'*

El Lissitzky's lecture on 'Design of the Book' was reported in BRIGADA KHUDOZHNIKOV NO 4 (1931) under the title of DO NOT SEPARATE FORM FROM CONTENT! He is recorded as saying: *'The old book was constructed for the ear, for silent reading from left to right, from top to bottom. Now the book is a unity of acoustics and optics.'* Furthermore, *'The book must be the unified work of the author and designer'*: sentiments identical to those of Theo Van Doesberg and de Stijl, upon whom Lissitzky had a significant influence.

Valéry may have thought that *'Advertising has annihilated the most powerful adjectives,'* yet it had a positive influence on the development of new typefaces and, as a model for new visual forms for poetry was influential on Mallarmé and the Russian Futurists, as we have seen. And when Wyndham Lewis came to publish BLAST in 1914, it was set in *grotesque* advertising headline type. No commercial London printer would accept the commission; Lewis had to bribe an alcoholic ex-printer with an ample supply of spirits to see the project through.

Three years later, Apollinaire was predicting that along with the advent of the new technology of film and recording, printing too had a potential for an unprecedented expressiveness, as *'typography had reached the last brilliant phase of its career'.* In his 1917 lecture, L'ESPRIT NOUVEAU ET LES POÈTES, he said: *'Typographic gimmicks, handled with great daring, have the advantage of giving rise to a visual lyricism which was virtually unknown to previous generations. These tricks and devices can go even further and achieve a synthesis of the arts, of music, painting, and literature.'* Believing in the 'simultaneity' of vision, Apollinaire propounded an art of expression which would enable the reader *'to read a whole poem at a single glance; just as a conductor reads the superimposed notes in a musical score all at once, so one can see the plastic and printed elements.'*

With this in mind, it is perhaps surprising that Apollinaire did not concern himself overmuch with the typographic presentation of his *Calligrammes*. Stefan Themerson has related how when he examined some proofs of Apollinaire's *Calligrammes* he found that though they were heavily corrected in black ink, the corrections were concerned only with spelling or word changes. No marks were made concerning either typeface or layout.

Four years before Apollinaire's pronouncements on the *'the last brilliant phase'* of typography Blaise Cendrars had developed new poetic techniques which objectified the word and gave typography a greater role in the concept of the text. Form and content may not always be so inevitably combined as in Apollinaire's IL PLEUT, with its characters drizzling down the page like droplets of rain, but the aim of the 'typographic' poet is always to seek an analogy between content, sonority and visual form. To this end for his first 'simultaneous' book, PROSE DU TRANSSIBÉRIEN ET DE LA PETITE JEHANNE DE FRANCE, Cendrars utilised as many different characters as he could find at the Crété printing works to set the text in more than ten disparate typefaces and sizes, attempting to orchestrate an expressive *vers libre* 'score', unified by Sonia Delaunay's artwork, itself printed in 80 different colours by the *pochoir* process.

In his essay THE POEM IN THE EYE (1975) the American poet John Hollander emphasised the importance of typographic layout as part of poetic language: *'A poem's shape, then, may be a frame for itself as it may be a frame for a picture of the world'.* Obviously, the visible disposition of words or sentences is an expressive element in printed language. *'Form,'* remarked the poet Charles Olson, *'is never more than extension of content'.* Both handwriting and printing he saw as obstructions to communication; print petrified the metrical line of spoken verse and erected a barrier between the poet and his audience. Olson's means to unify the material signifier with the conceptual, emotional and spiritual signified was the intermediate technology of the typewriter: *'due to its rigidity and its space precisions, it can, for a poet, indicate exactly the breath, the pauses, the suspensions even of syllables, the juxtapositions even of parts of phrases, which he intends. For the first time the poet has the stave and the bar a musician has had.'*

'Concrete poetry', the only *international* poetry movement, has in recent years increased our awareness of the letter as object and of the word as form in space. The concrete poet's acceptance of the word as a group of letters, potentially non-semantic, has led to the liberation also of the letter itself; the visual form of both has been realized as expressive, and what Edwin Morgan has called *'a jolt into perception'* has occurred.

'... this will increasingly affect publishing, education, art training, and many forms of design, quite apart from the impact on aesthetics itself. There will be no more double-column Spensers with every line turned over because there is 'no space' for it. And perhaps we shall now get Ezra Pound's famous little haiku IN A STATION OF THE METRO printed as he intended it (and as it never is):

The apparition   of these faces   in the crowd:

Petals   on a wet, black   bough:

Poets have been the slaves of publishers and printers for too long. They are now beginning to assert themselves.'

Yet the typographer may still play a positive role. In a poem such as Pound's, syntactic discontinuity can be recognised and given value through sensitive typographic treatment. Its visual identity may be considered a factor in the process of oral transmission; as Pound himself wrote: *'All typographic disposition, placing of words on the page, is intended to facilitate the readers intonation, whether he be reading silently or aloud to friends.'* As we have seen, it is also a visual entity in itself.

The report on El Lissitzky is reprinted in EL LISSITZKY 1890-1941 exhibition catalogue, *Harvard University Arts Museums/Busch Reisinger Museum, 1987*

Guillaume Apollinaire, L'ESPRIT NOUVEAU ET LES POÈTES, published in *Mercure de France, 1 Dec 1918,* quoted in Massin, LETTER AND IMAGE, *Studio Vista, London, 1970*

John Hollander, VISION AND ROMANCE: TWO SENSES OF THE POETIC FORM, *Oxford University Press, New York, 1975*

Robert Creeley (ed), SELECTED WRITINGS OF CHARLES OLSON, *New Directions, New York, 1966*

Edwin Morgan, 'Into the constellation', in AKROS, vol 6 no 18, *March 1972*

Ezra Pound is quoted from a letter to Hubert Creekmore, February 1939, in EZRA POUND, ed J P Sullivan, *Penguin Critical Anthologies, London, 1970*

Aldous Huxley, 'Introduction' to Oliver Simon and Julius Rodenberg's PRINTING OF TODAY, *Peter Davis Ltd, 1928*

Bruce Rogers, PARAGRAPHS ON PRINTING, *William E Rudge's Sons, New York, 1943,* reprinted *1979, Dover Publications, NY*

Paul Beaujon (Beatrice Warde), in MONOTYPE RECORDER, 35, 2, *Summer 1936*

Stephane Mallarmé, 'Le Livre, Instrument Spirituel', published in REVUE BLANCHE *1 July 1895*

Stefan Themerson, 'Ideogrammes Lyriques' in TYPOGRAPHIA (New Series) *December 1975;* and 'Wooff Wooff, or Who Killed Richard Wagner' *1951* reprinted in ON SEMANTIC POETRY, *Gaberbocchus, London, 1975*

F T Marinetti, MANIFESTO OF FUTURISM in *Le Figaro,* 20 February, 1909 quoted in Herbert Spencer PIONEERS OF MODERN TYPOGRAPHY, *Lund Humphries, 1969*

From El Lissitzky's designs for Mayakovsky's *For Reading Aloud,* 1923

LA COLOMBE POIGNARDÉE
ET LE JET D'EAU

Douces figures poignardées Chères lèvres fleuries
MIA   MAREYE
  YETTE   LORIE
  ANNIE   et toi   MARIE
       où   êtes
          vous   ô
          jeunes   filles
              MAIS
           près d'un
          jet d'eau qui
         pleure et qui prie
       cette colombe s'extasie

Tous les souvenirs de naguère
O mes amis partis en guerre
Jaillissent vers le firmament
Et vos regards en l'eau dormant
Meurent mélancoliquement

Où sont-ils Braque et Max Jacob
Derain aux yeux gris comme l'aube

Où sont Raynal Billy Dalize
Dont les noms se mélancolisent
Comme des pas dans une église
Où est Cremnitz qui s'engagea
Peut-être sont-ils mort déjà
De souvenirs mon âme est pleine
Le jet d'eau pleure sur ma peine

CEUX QUI SONT PARTIS A LA GUERRE AU NORD SE BATTENT MAINTENANT
Le soir tombe O sanglante mer
Jardins où saigne abondamment le laurier rose fleur guerrière

Apollinaire, *calligramme*

98

LES VERS FIGURÉS

DANS L'ANTIQUITÉ ET AU MOYEN ÂGE

Simmias de Rhodes vivait sous le règne de Ptolémée Lagide, vers 325 avant l'ère chrétienne. Médiocre poète, autant qu'on en puisse juger par les quelques épigrammes qui lui sont attribuées, il est probable que son nom serait tombé dans l'oubli, s'il ne lui était venu l'étrange idée de donner à ses vers la figure des objets qu'il voulait décrire. De ces petites compositions que l'on nomme des *vers figurés*, trois nous ont été conservées par la *Couronne de Méléagre*. Ce sont les *Ailes*, l'*Œuf*, la *Hache*. Les *Ailes* sont composées chacune de six plumes ou de six vers, qui diminuent graduellement de mesure, et par conséquent de longueur, selon leur position dans l'aile. Simmias y fait parler l'Amour, le dieu qui porte des ailes, non point le fils de Vénus, mais cet antique Amour que chantent les cosmogonies, le principe créateur et contemporain du Destin :

« Regarde-moi : je suis le roi de la terre immense, et j'ai chassé du ciel l'Acmonide. Ne t'étonne pas de ce que, paraissant aussi jeune, mes joues sont ombragées d'une barbe épaisse : c'est que je suis né sous le règne d'Ananké, lorsqu'à la sombre domination de la Terre obéissaient les animaux, ceux de l'air et ceux de l'Océan. Je ne suis pas le fils de Cypris, j'ai des ailes rapides et l'on m'appelle l'Amour éthéré. Ce n'est pas par la force que je domine, je triomphe par la persuasion. La terre, l'abîme des mers, le ciel d'airain, tout m'obéit ; je leur ai enlevé l'antique sceptre, et les dieux mêmes reconnaissent ma voix. » (Trad. Dehèque).

La composition de l'*Œuf* a exigé beaucoup plus de patience. Chaque bout est formé de très petits vers qui s'allongent progressivement jusqu'au milieu. Ces vers sont de différents mètres ; et l'auteur, qui n'y épargnait point sa peine, a choisi, au dire de l'helléniste Boissonade, les plus embarrassants et les moins ordinaires des mètres. Mais ce n'est pas tout : le poème, tel qu'il se présente, est absurde, inintelligible, c'est une énigme indéchiffrable. Il faut, pour trouver une espèce de sens, aller du premier vers au dernier, du second à l'avant-dernier, du troisième à l'antépénultième, et ainsi de suite jusqu'aux deux vers du milieu. Un ancien scholiaste, découvert par Saumaise, nous a fort heureusement dévoilé ce merveilleux artifice. La figure des vers en a décidé le sujet. C'est un œuf de rossignol dorien que le poète offre aux lecteurs : Mercure l'a pris sous les ailes de la mère pour le donner aux hommes :

« Œuvre d'une mère aux doux chants, prends cet œuf que vient de pondre un rossignol dorien. De bon cœur, reçois-le ; une harmonieuse mère l'a déposé dans le chaste nid de ses amours. Le messager des dieux à la voix sonore, Mercure l'a lancé parmi les hommes, l'ayant pris sous l'aile de sa mère. Il a voulu que les vers, d'une seule mesure d'abord, s'allongeassent jusqu'au dixième vers, paré des ornements du rythme ; et par delà dirigeant l'allure oblique et rapide des mesures diverses, il a, du pied, marqué la cadence du chant varié et symétrique des Muses, rivalisant de vitesse avec des faons, petits des cerfs rapides. Ceux qu'aiguillonnent la faim et l'amour, courent vers la mamelle de leur mère, s'élançant d'une course impétueuse par-dessus les hauts sommets, sur les traces de leur nourrice

BAUDELAIRE
L'ÉTRANGER

Qui

aimes-tu le mieux, homme énigmatique, dis ?

TA MÈRE   TA SŒUR

TON PÈRE   TON FRÈRE   ?

Je n'ai ni père, ni mère,
ni sœur, ni frère.

TES AMIS ?

Vous vous servez là d'une parole
dont le sens m'est resté jusqu'à ce jour
inconnu

TA PATRIE ?

J'ignore sous quelle latitude
elle est située

LA BEAUTÉ ?

Je l'aimerais volontiers, **DÉESSE** *et*
IMMORTELLE

l'OR ?

Je le hais
comme vous haïssez DIEU

Eh! qui aimes-tu donc,
extraordinaire étranger

?

J'AIME les nuages...
les NUAGES qui passent...
Là-bas... LA-BAS...

les merveilleux nuages!

FREGIO MECANO

(Carattere scomponibile)

Minimo Kg. 2,50   Si vendono anche figure separate: minimo Kg. 1 per figura

This remarkable typeface was designed by an unknown Italian in the 1920s. Every letter of the alphabet, and all the numerals, can be made using combinations of the twenty segments shown here.

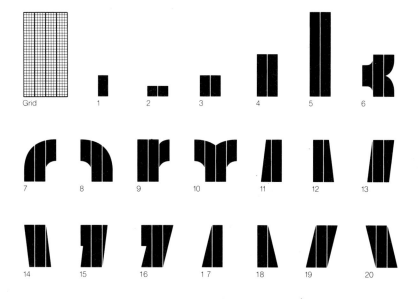

The segments join to form a letter with the joints expressed as a white line. The vertical white lines create a pattern which unifies the letter. It is possible to create a serif alphabet simply by adding segments.

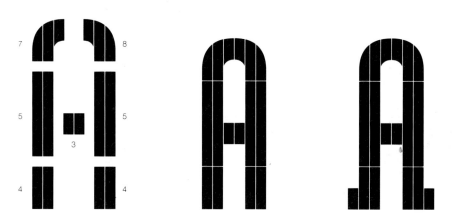

By increasing the number of segments used, the letters can assume extreme forms. Letters can be created to occupy any kind of space. The real ingenuity is that from twenty pieces an infinite number of alphabets are possible.

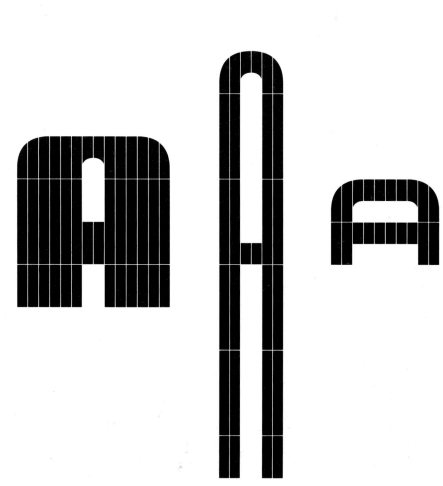

School of decorative Art, Stuttgart, Professor Veit. Signets
composed of brass rules and typographical borders.

TYPOGRAPHICAL SIGNETS

abcdefghijk
lmnopqrſstu
unxyz
aaaaaaß

This type is set with typographical material (Brass Rule). The letter ‹a› below shows how the individual pieces are assembled.

graphische abteilung der württembergischen staatlichen

A specimen showing the possibilities in letter formation

kunstgewerbeschule stuttgart

School of decorative Art, Stuttgart. Brass Rule Letters

CONSTRUCTED LETTERS

日刊ゲンダイ

89. 5. 18

71

18線

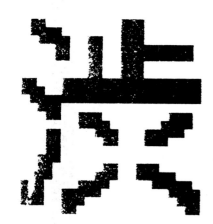

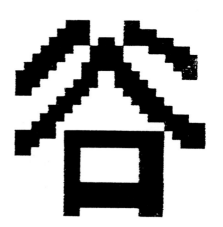

峰村東即殿

S20125

2個口

月木B版

50部

Label used on newspaper package, Tokyo

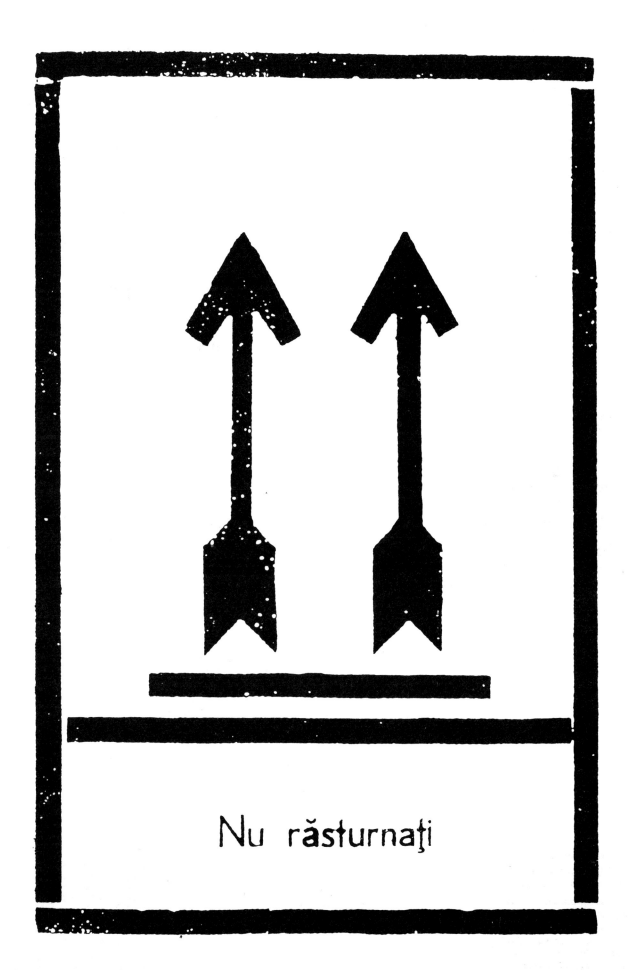

Nu răsturnaţi

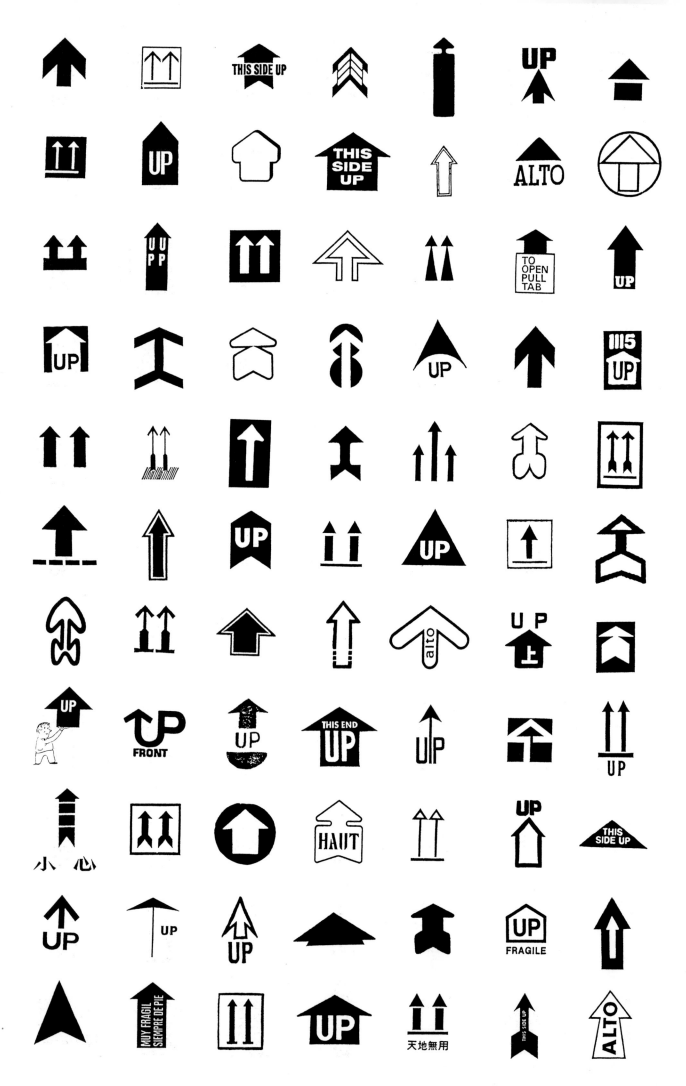

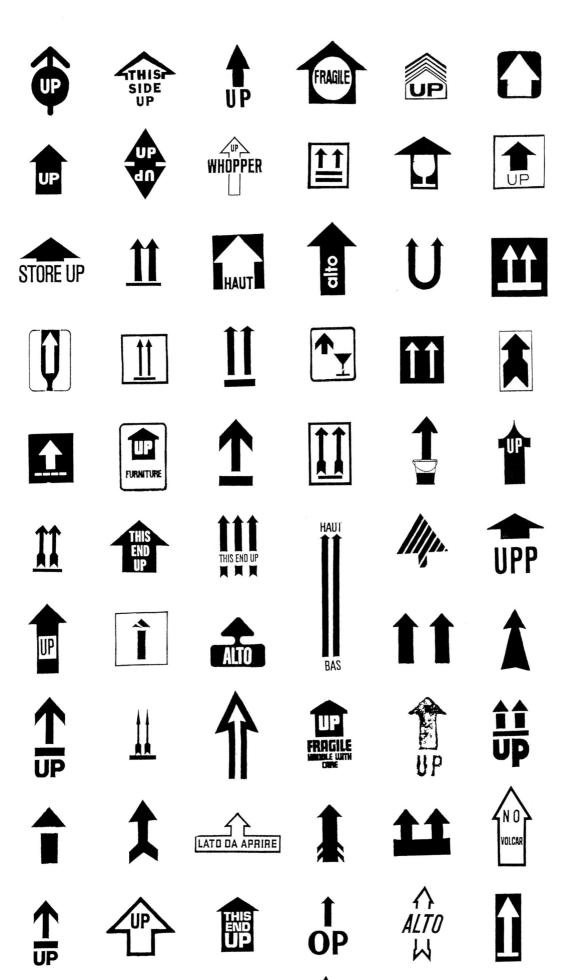

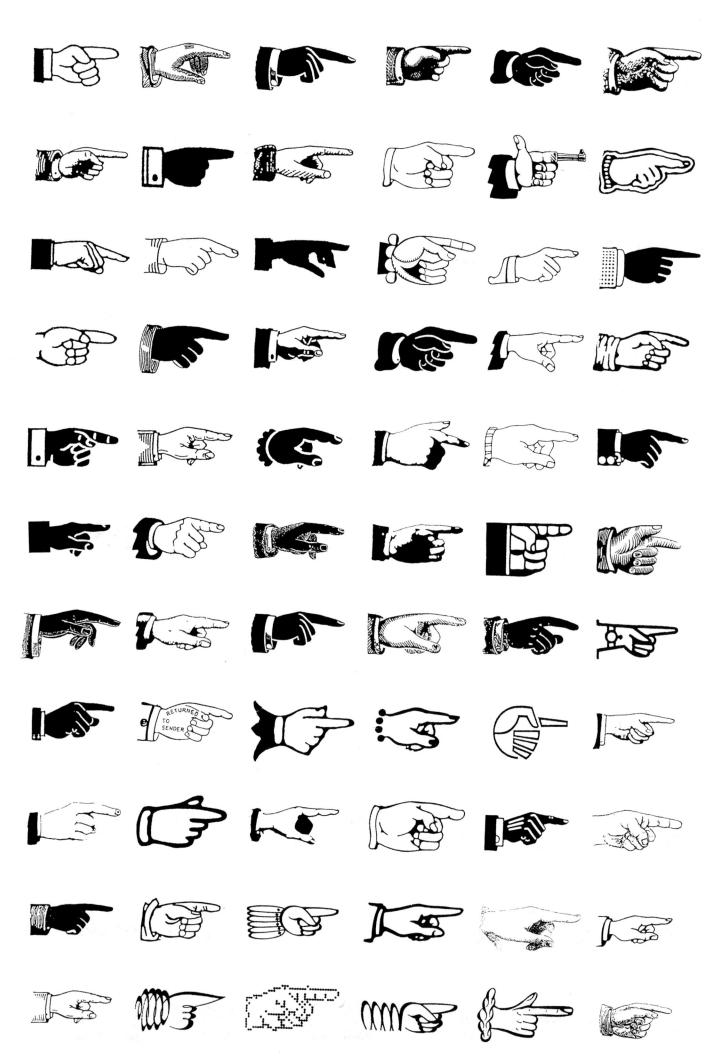

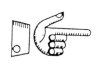    

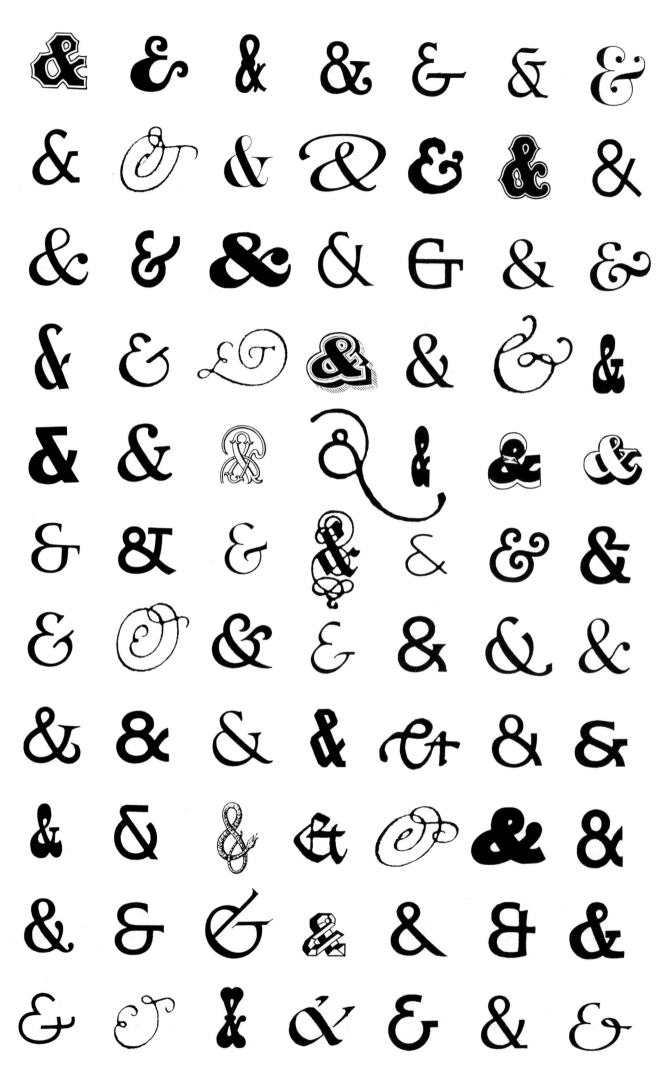

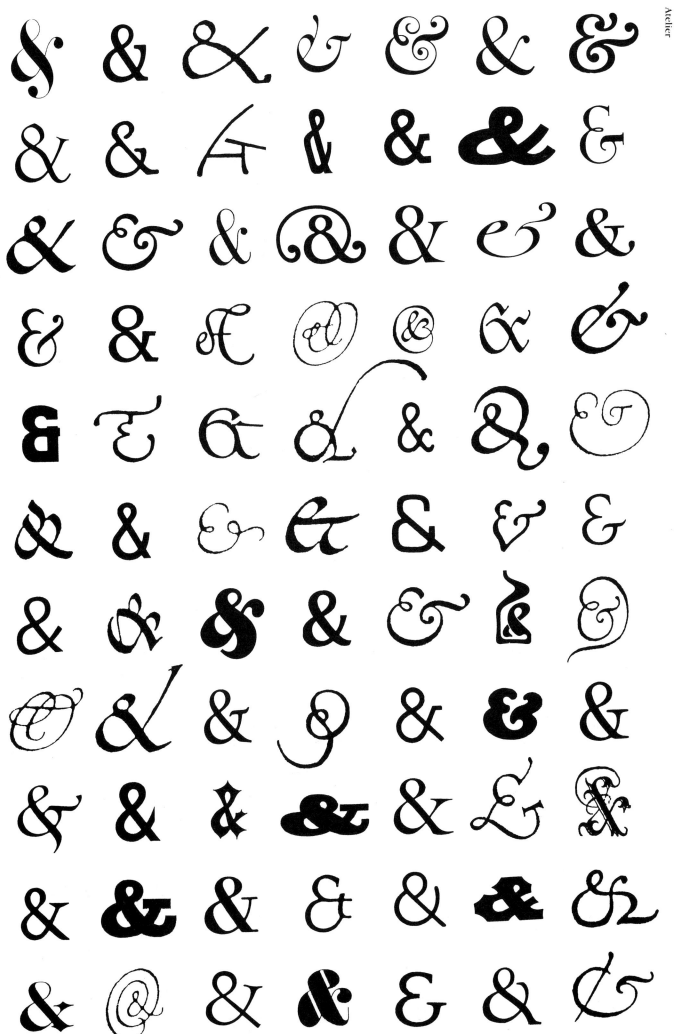

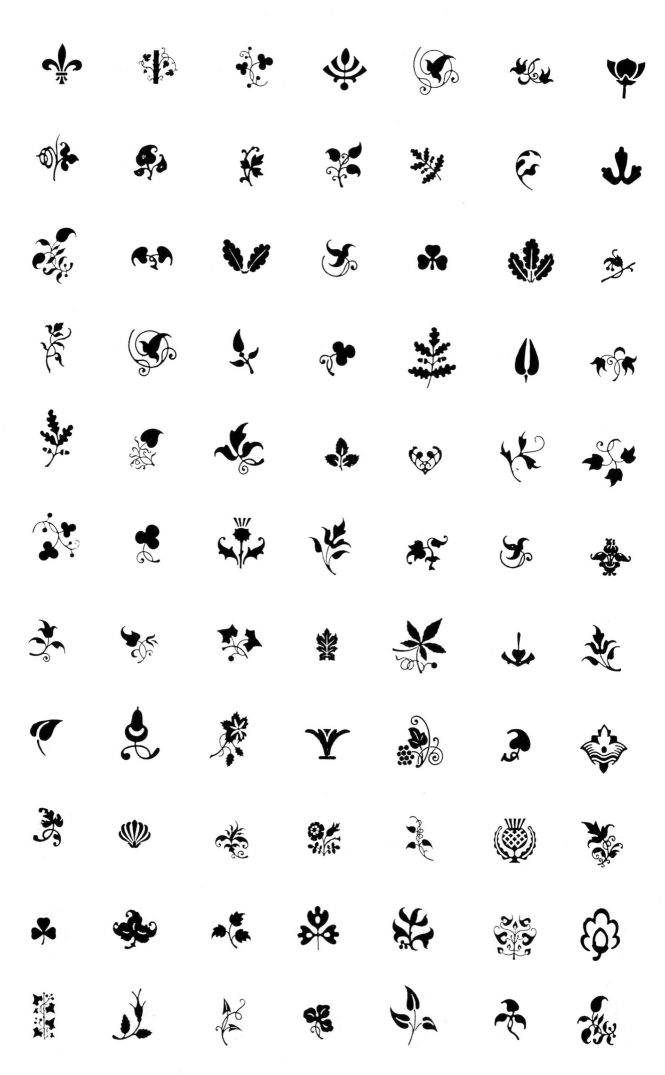

114

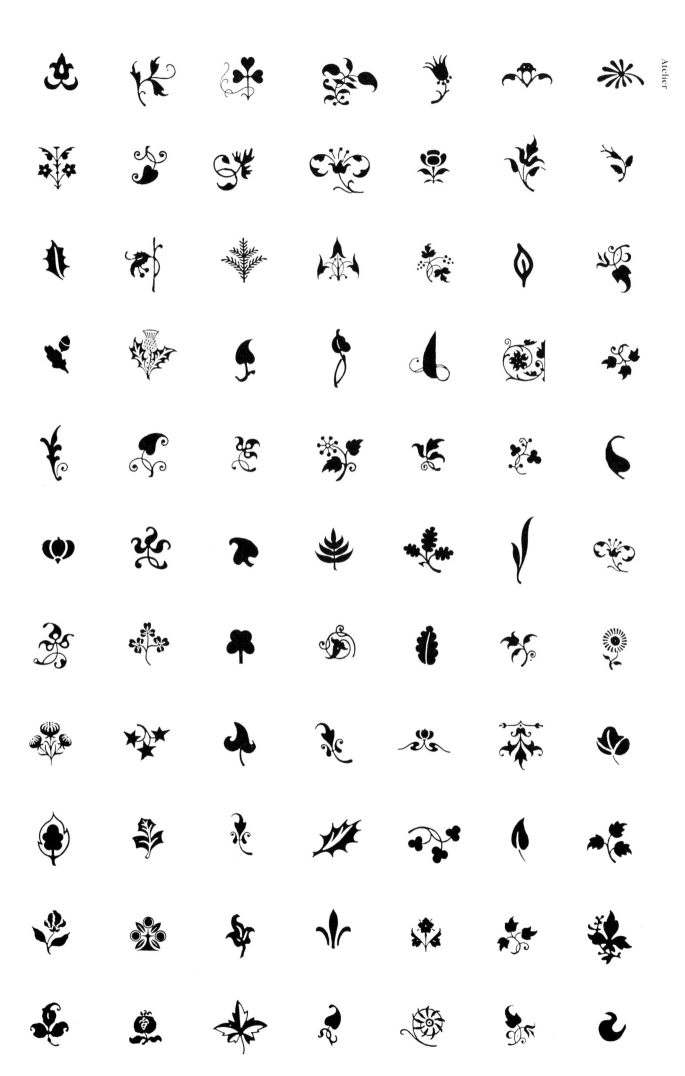

BESTE SORTE № 3

SCHMI

S. OPPENHEIM & Co.
SCHMIRGELWERK.

RGELLEINEN.

Schmale Jonisch.

ABCDEF
GHIJKLMN
OPQRSTUV
WXYZ

Schriftgiesserei Genzsch & Heyse, Hamburg.

Schattierte Jonisch.

A B C D E F G H I
J K L M N O P Q R S T
U V W X Y Z
a b c d e f g h i j k l m n o
p q r s t u v v w x y z
1 2 3 4 5 6 7 8 9 0

Schriftgiesserei Flinsch, Frankfurt a. M.

Halbfette Egyptienne.

ABCDEFGHIJ
KLMNOPQRSTU
VWXYZ
abcdefghijklmno
pqrstuvwxyz

Schriftgiesserei Bauer & Comp., Stuttgart.

Lichte Jonisch.

ABCDE
FGHIJK
LMNOP
QRSTUV
WXYZ

Schriftgiesserei Jul. Klinkhardt, Leipzig.

Kursiv.

A B C D E F G H I
J K L M N O P Q R S
T U V W X Y Z
a b c d e f g h i j k l m n
o p q r s t u v v w x y z
1 2 3 4 5 6 7 8 9 0

Schriftgiesserei Schelter & Giesecke, Leipzig.

Breite Egyptienne.

ABCDEFGHIJKLMNO
PQRSTUVWWXYZ
abcdefghijklmnnopqrstu
vwwxyz
1234567890

Breite (geschweifte) Italienne.

A B C D E F G H I J
K L M N O P Q R S
T U V W X Y Z
1 2 3 4 5 6
7 8 9 0

Schriftgiesserei von Gensch & Heyse in Hamburg.

Italienne Kursiv.

A B C D E F G H I J
K L M N O P Q R S T U
V W X Y Z
a b c d e f g h i j k l m n o p
q r s t u v w x y z
1 2 3 4 5 6 7 8 9 0

Schriftgiesserei von Scholer & Giesecke in Leipzig.

Schattierte Italienne.

A B C D E F G H I J K L
M N O P Q R S T U V W
a b c d e f X Y Z g h i j k l
m n o p q r s t u v w x y z

Schriftgiesserei Flinsch in Frankfurt a. M.

Italienne.

A B C D E F G
M N O P Q R
X Y Z
1 2 3 4 5 6
7 8 9 0

Schriftgiesserei von Gensch & Heyse in Hamburg.

Italienne Kursiv.

A B C D E F G H
I J K L M N O P Q R
S T U V W X Y Z

Schriftgiesserei von Julius Klinkhardt in Leipzig.

Breite Italienne.

A B C D E F G H I J K L M N
O P Q R S T U V W X Y Z
a b c d e f g h i j k l m n o p q r s t u
v w x y z
1 2 3 4 5 6 7 8 9 0

Schriftgiesserei von Scholer & Giesecke in Leipzig.

ABCDEFGHIJKLMNOPQRS
12345 TUVWXYZ 67890
abcdefghijklmnopqrstuvwxyz

Richard BREMEN Wagner

Schriftgiesserei von Bauer & Comp. in Stuttgart.

Breite verzierte Clarendon.

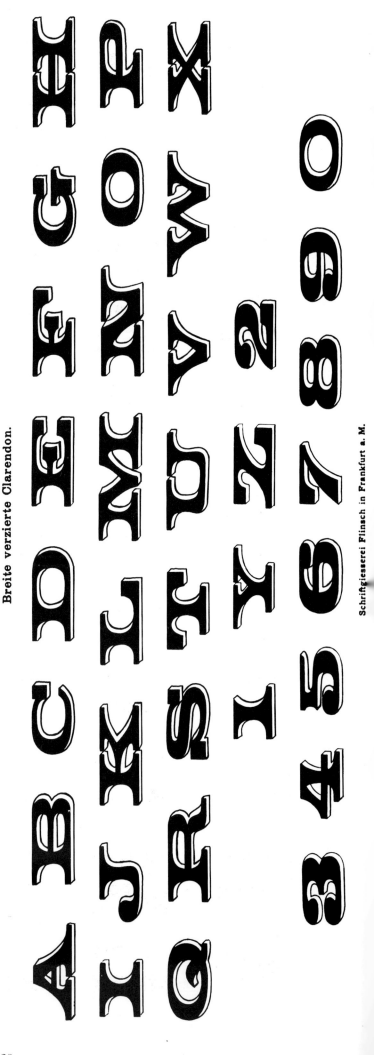

Schriftgiesserei Flinsch in Frankfurt a. M.

A B C D E F G H I J K
L M N O P Q R S T U V
1 2 3 4 5 W X Y Z 6 7 8 9 0
a b c d e f g h i k l m n o
p q r s t u v w x y z

Handsome letters from a specimen book – Petzendorfer, Schriften-Atlas, Stuttgart.

ABCDEFG HIJKL
MNOPQRSTUVW
XYZ123456789

Antiqua.

ABCDEFGHIJKLMN
OPQRSTUVWXYZ
abcdefghijklmnopqrst
12345uvwxyz67890

ABCDEFGHIJKLMNOPQ
RSTUVWXYZ
abcdefghijklmnopqrstuvwxyz
1234567890

ABCDEFGHIJK
LMNOPQRSTU
VWXYZ
abcdefghiklmnopqr
stuvwxyz
1234567890

ABCDEFGHIJ
KLMNOPQRST
UVWXYZ
abcdefghijk
lmnopqrstuv
wxyz

ABCDEFGHIJ
KLMNOPQRST
UVWXYZ
abcdefghijklm
nopqrstuvwxyz
1234567890

ABCDEFGHIJKLMNOPQRSTUV
WXYZ 1234567890
abcdefghijklmnopqrstuvwxyz
Hamburg BRESLAU München

THE DIRECTLY-USEFUL D.U. TECHNICAL SERIES

HAND LETTERING

Modern Roman Italic Capitals :   In alphabetical order and correctly spaced :   Pencil and Ink Exercises.   PLATE 3.

.5" { abcdefghijklmnopq } 1"

.4" { rstuvwxyz. abcdefghi } .8"

68°

1234567890.1234
567890.1234567890.12
34567890.1234567890.12

.5"

.45"

Modern Roman Italic Figures :   In numerical order and correctly spaced :   Pencil and Ink Exercises.   PLATE 4.

125

ABCDEFGHIJKL
MNOPQRSTUVW
XYZ. 1234567890.&

ABCDEFGHIJKL
MNOPQRSTUVW
XYZ. 12345678

Modern Roman Vertical Capitals : Alphabetically and numerically arranged, and correctly spaced : Ink. PLATE 67.

126

TURKEY IN ASIA

.8"

THE WORLD

.75"

MERCATOR'S PROJECTION

SKETCH FOR A PORTION

.65"

.6"

DINING ROOM OF THE

OF THE

.3"

PALAZZO REZZONICO, VENICE.

.5"

Modern Roman Vertical Capitals :

Words arranged continuously :

Ink Exercises.

PLATE 68.

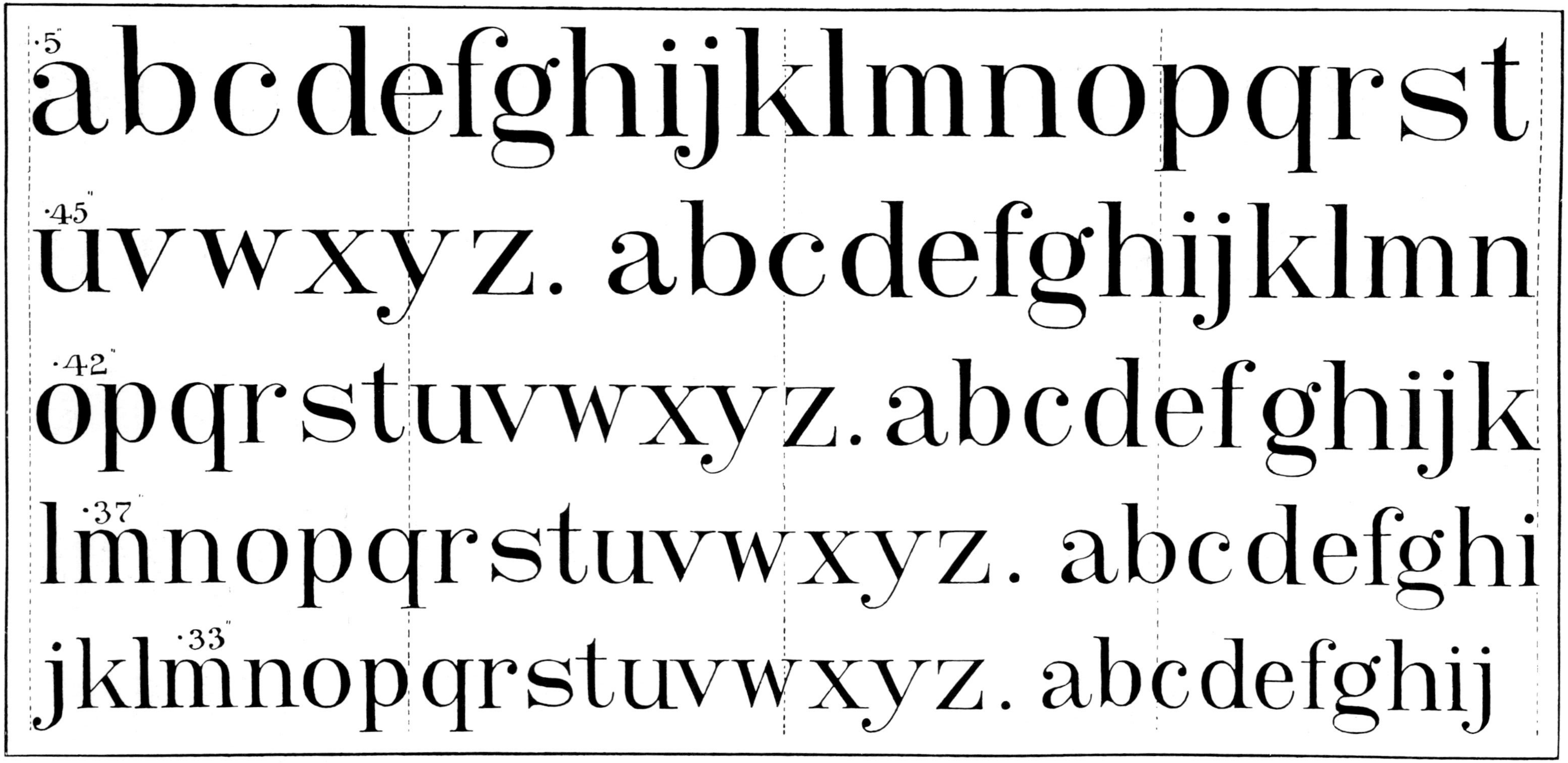

.5 abcdefghijklmnopqrst

.45" tuvwxyz. abcdefghijklmn

.42" opqrstuvwxyz. abcdefghijk

1.37" lmnopqrstuvwxyz. abcdefghi

.33" jklmnopqrstuvwxyz. abcdefghij

Modern Roman Vertical Smalls :   In alphabetical order and correctly spaced :   Ink Exercises.   PLATE 72.

ABCDEFGHIJKL
MNOPQRSTUVW

Variant

[R]

XYZ.1234567890.

ABCDEFGHIJKLMNOP
QRSTUVWXYZ.1234567

.8"

.75"

.7"

.6"

.5"

Old Roman or Renaissance :

Alphabets and Figures.

PLATE 91.

129

.65

ABCDEFGHIJKLMN
OPQRSTUVWXYZ&

.65

ABCDEFGHIJKLMN
OPQRSTUVWXYZ&
234567890.23456789.

Use of Stencils :

Showing mode of hand-finishing where underlined.

PLATE 103.

130

ABCDEFGHIJKLMNOPQRS
TUVWXYZ&234567890.;Y

abcdefghijklmnopqrstuvwxyz.-

ABCDEFGHIJKLMNOPQR
STUVWXYZ&1234567890

abcdefghijklmnopqrstuvwxyz.V

Thick Block Vertical Capitals, Figures, and Smalls :
Thick Block Vertical Capitals, Figures, and Smalls, Serif-relieved :

In alphabetical order and correctly spaced.   PLATE 84.

131

Natalia Goncharova, front and back cover for THE CITY by Alexander Roubakine, 1920

ПАРИЖЪ
1920

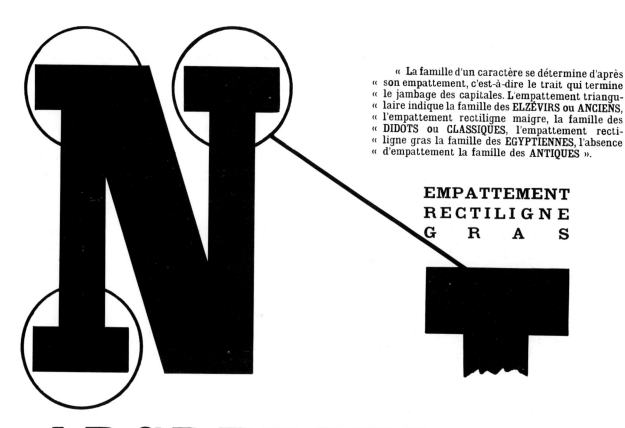

EMPATTEMENT
RECTILIGNE
G R A S

ABCDEFGHIJKLM
NOPQRSTUVWXYZ

abcdefghijklm
nopqrstuvwxyz

1234567890

TYPE D'EGYPTIENNE : LA COMPACTE

L'ART DE RECONNAITRE UN CARACTÈRE
(PRINCIPE DE THIBAUDEAU)

ABCDEFGHI
JKLMNOPQR
STUVWXYZ&
abcdefghijklmn
opqrstuvwxyz

‹CONCORDIA› · BAUER & CO. · STUTTGART & H. BERTHOLD · BERLIN

ABCDEFGHIJKLMNOPQR
12345 · STUVWXYZ · 67890
abcdefghijklmnopqrstu
HELVETIA · vwxyz · DOCUMENT
Calame · Renaissance · Gladstone

CARACTÈRE A DEUX CHASSES

AA B CC DD
EE FF G HH
I J K LL M
NN O PP Q
RR SS TT UU
V W X Y Z
Æ Œ Ç & Cⁱᵉ
( ) . , ; : ' - « » ! ?
1 2 3 4 5 6 7 8 9 0

SOMMAIRE

NUMÉRO

51

Louis CHÉRONNET :
A propos du "Narcisse" de Paul Valéry, illustré par Laure-Albin Guillot   5

Maurice BARRET :
Foire ou Exposition? Leçon et avertissement pour l'Exposition 1937.   9

Jacques DUPONT :
Quelques dessins flamands   19

Pierre NORIEY :
Cartes romantiques de vœux   25

Marie DORMOY :
Monotypes de Degas   33

Mathilde LEFOURNIER :
Le Ski millénaire   39

René SERVANT :
Notions de couleurs pour servir en trichromie (fin)   43

Rémy DUVAL :
Herbert Matter   44

Pietro SARDELLA :
Le livre italien au XVe siècle   51

Alphabet gothique   56

Arnold SUTER :
La Mésaventure de l'Abbé Domenech.   58

Actualités   60

Échos   69

HORS-TEXTE

Feuille d'étude de Jérôme Bosch . . . .   22^1

Quelques cartes romantiques de la collection Sack . . . .   32^1

Étude de Léon Gischia (procédé Uhl) . . . .   38^1

Couverture de l'Annuaire 1936 du Ski Club de Paris . . .   50^1

Dépliant de la Cie des chemins de fer fédéraux suisses et carte de vœux de l'imprimerie Otto Kösler . . .   60^1

Planche extraite de la revue Matford . . . . . .   62^1

15 FÉVRIER 1936

ARTS ET MÉTIERS GRAPHIQUES

EXCLUSIVE AGENT FOR U. S. A.

FRENCH AND EUROPEAN PUBLICATIONS, Inc.

610, FIFTH AVENUE, NEW-YORK N. Y.

DIRECTEUR
CHARLES PEIGNOT
RÉDACTION:
ANDRÉ LEJARD

CONFÉRENCE
13456789

ÉLECTRICITÉ
123567

PAQUEBOT

NUIT DE
SOIN
CRÉDIT
FERME

Date
Lac
CID

APPARTEMENTS

CONFECTION

INITIALES SIMPLES LARGES 3ᵉ Catégorie.

COUR
BISE

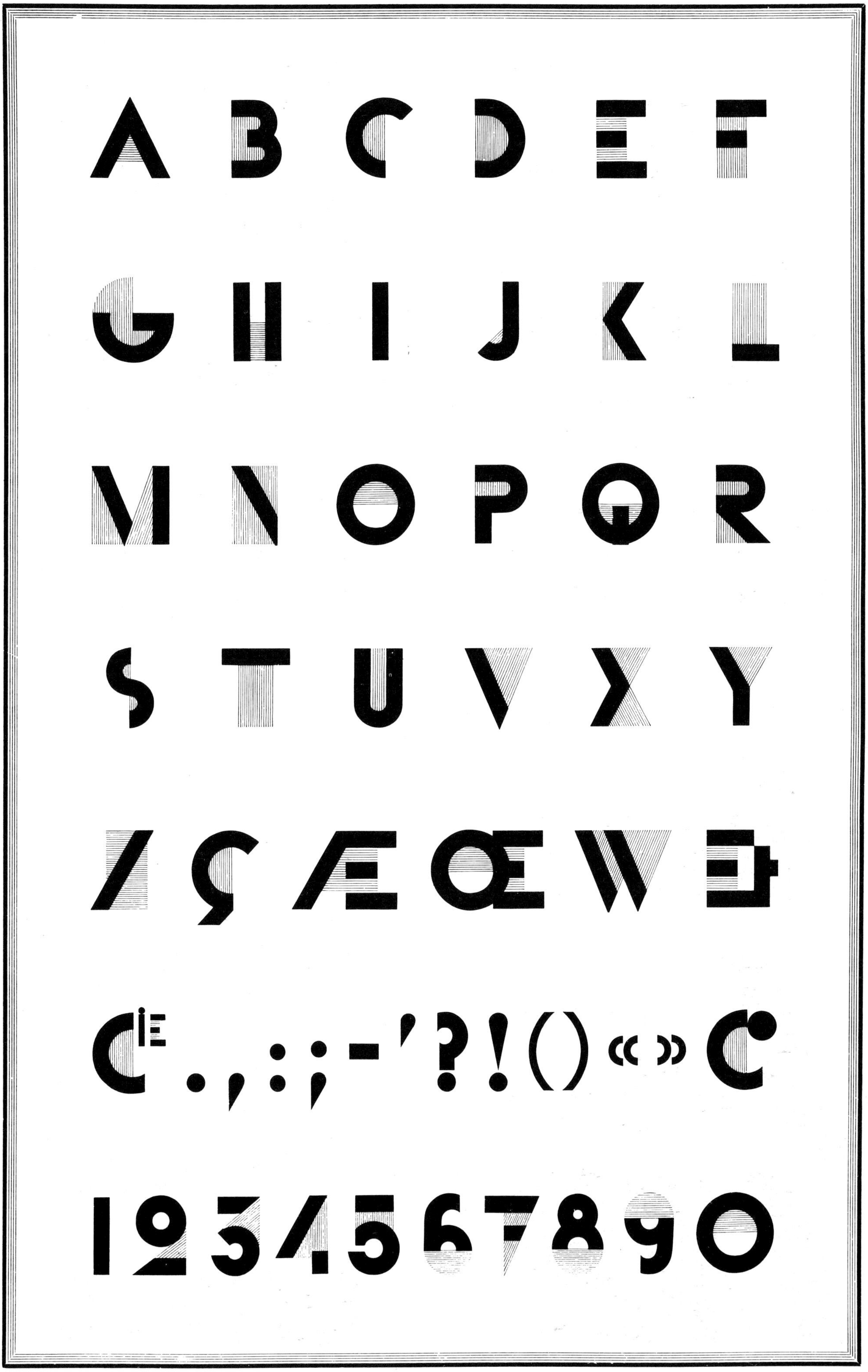

A B C D E F
G H I J K L
M N O P Q R
S T U V X Y
/ S Æ Œ W Þ
Ç .,.:;-'?!()«»Ç
1 2 3 4 5 6 7 8 9 0

FONDERIES DEBERNY & PEIGNOT, 18, RUE FERRUS, PARIS

ABCDEFG
HIJKLMNO
PQRSTU
VWXYZ
,,,'"" -!?
£1234567
890&℃°

TRENTE
ANS

OU LA VIE
D'UN JOUEUR
DE POLO

THE
ANCHOR
TEA-ROOM
HENDAYE

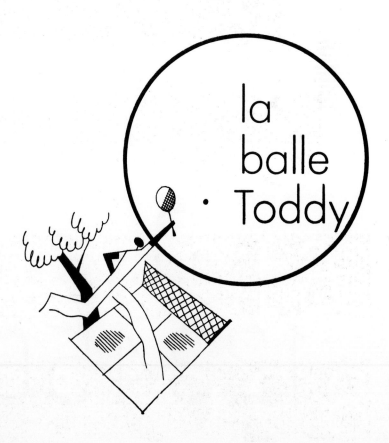

la
balle
Toddy

FASHION CONDENSED

ABCDEFGHI
JKLMNOPQRS
TUVWXYZ

&.,.;-'''!?
1234567890

RIBBONETTE

A B C D E F G H I J

K L M N O P Q R S

S T U V W X Y Z &

$ ¢

1 2 3 4 5 6 7 8 9 0

. , : ; - ' " " ! ?

ABCDEFGHI
JKLMNOPQR
STUVWXYZ
& Œ Æ 1234

1234567890

1234567890

1234567890

GOTHIC.

IIIIIIIVVVIVIIVIIIIXX

9TH CENTURY.

1234567890

14TH CENTURY.

1234567890

1470.

AD 1554

12TH CENTURY.

1234567890

15TH CENTURY.

1234567890

13TH CENTURY.

123456789

16TH CENTURY.

1234567890

144

EXCELSIOR ZWICKY

AU CYGNE

H K

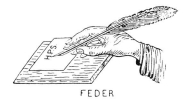

FEDER

SOLTEX ZEGNA

PASTA SPECIALE al PURO UOVO

"la Perfetta"

Industria Paste Alimentari

Cav. Luigi Sesti

LUCCA Italy

STAB. CORTI & C. LIVORNO

EXCELSIOR ZWICKY

ARBEITE, SAMMLE, VERMEHRE!

MARQUE DÉPOSÉE

DEGEA

PASTA SPECIALE al PURO UOVO

OLYMPIA

MARCA DEPOS

FABBRICATO DA S.A. BORGHI-MILANO

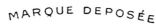

MARQUE DEPOSÉE

AUX DEUX LOUFERS

REGISTERED TRADE MARK

1799
HÜCKEL
„Durit"

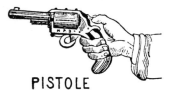

PISTOLE

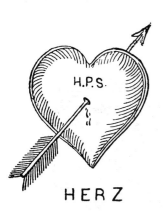

H.P.S.

HERZ

DEPOSITATA

T A N K

SCOPIFICIO - DEGHESE

MARCA

D & G
DEGO

CAMPEADOR
ED. PINAUD
PARIS

EXTRA PUR

LA GUITARE

SEELIGMANN'S

SCHMIRGELPAPIER

GESETZLICH GESCHÜTZT.

GESETZLICH GESCHÜTZT.

Nº

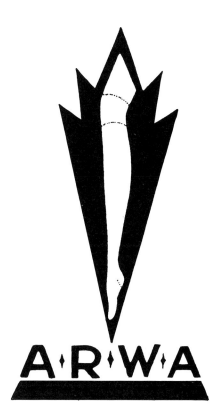

ARWA

MALÙ

ALCA

PINAUD "612"

GAMMA

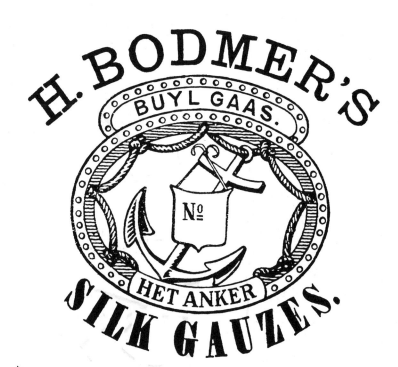

CHINA-PEDRONI

SPECIALITA

DELLA SOC.ª AN.ᵐᵉ

DISTILLERIE PEDRONI

MILANO

D.PETER, Inventeur

GALA PETER

CHOCOLAT AU LAIT

Calçado

ATLAS

ECKENDORFER

Original

Runkelsamen

Genau nach Photographie

SCHUTZ-MARKE

L'OLÉO

MARQUE

DÉPOSÉE

BOUGIE-OLÉO

MAGNETO

Huiles

Serpolleïne

OLÉOMOTO D

Les meilleurs lubrifiants connus pour AUTOMOBILES

Exiger l'Étui revêtu de cette Étiquette

SE MÉFIER   CONTREFAÇONS

ÉTIQUETTE DÉPOSÉE en FRANCE et à L'ÉTRANGER

PLAYING CARDS.

GREAT MOGUL

PLAYING CARDS.

DE L'ETABLISSEMENT DE

SAUL D. MODIANO TRIESTE

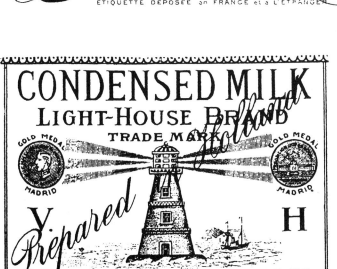

CONDENSED MILK

LIGHT-HOUSE BRAND

TRADE MARK

GOLD MEDAL MADRID

GOLD MEDAL MADRID

V. *Prepared* H

VAN HEEL'S MILK

★ **HAUS NEUERBURG** ★

ZIGARETTEN

ZIGARETTEN

HAUS NEUERBURG

25 LÖWENBRÜCK 25

"COLUMBUS"

LANGENBACH & SÖHNE / WORMS
HOFLIEFERANTEN

TELE FUN KEN

CEREALI E SEMI DA PRATO

ISOLTEX

MARCA DEPOSITATA

NAAMLOOZE VENNOOTSCHAP GOUDA
KAASHANDELMAATSCHAPPIJ
COPEKA
GOUDA (HOLLAND)

MAGLIERIE STERILIZZATE · THONSON ·

CYCLES
THOMANN
NANTERRE
SEINE

· LEOPARD ·

DÈPOSE
VOX HUMANA
DÈPOSE

ELECTRICUS

Sélecta

"VIGILANTE"

„ADAM & EVA"

ORIGINAL DIAMANT MANTLE

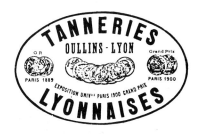

SCHWALBE

VITALDENT

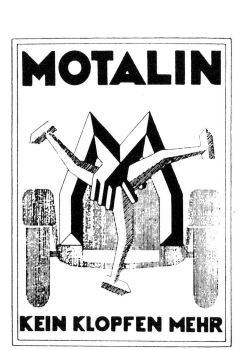

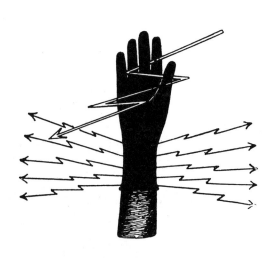

THÉ "ZÉBRA"

زبرة

MARQUE DÉPOSÉE

WADDINGTONS
BACCARAT
NO 3333
PLAYING CARDS

RIGHT STUFF
RS

RENOWNED GIN DISTILLERY
THE NETHERLANDS
DISTILLERIES
DELFT
HOLLAND

ABRASIVE
PRODUITS
ROTEX
PRODUCTS
ABRASIFS

F.L. Cailler

F.S.T.

FLOR DEL VINO NAVARRO

FIJNE OUDE HOLLANDSCHE
SCHIEDAM
J.D.K & Z.
JOHs DE KUYPER & ZOON
ROTTERDAM

A LA JONQUE CHINOISE

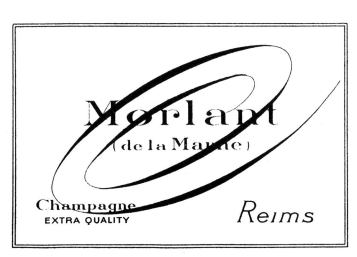

Morlant
(de la Marne)
Champagne
EXTRA QUALITY
Reims

SIDRA ESPUMOSA
FLOR DE
ASTURIAS
MARCA REGISTRADA
Avila y Gutierrez
AVILÉS ESPAÑA
Póngase la botella en posición horizontal

EXTRA
ORANGES
VALENCIA
M.K.

Esportazione Agrumi

THE LITTLE SELLER

FRUIT EXPORTER

BENEDETTO SCIORTINO & C:

Oranges de grand luxe

SIMAT   ALARIO   VALENCE
Les plus douces et exquises
de Valence et du Monde

JOSE MARTINEZ TORTONDA

JACINTO   ESPAGNE
ORANGES SUPERIEURES

A BON ARBRE
BON FRUIT

SIMAT

ALARIO

TRANQUILINO TORNERO

MURCIA

ROSITA ADSUARA

ALMAZORA

BAUTISTA PEREZ

EXTRA   ORANGES
SELECTED
LOS VALLES

Maniera bizzarra di esprimere le Figure Aritmetiche con Comiche positure

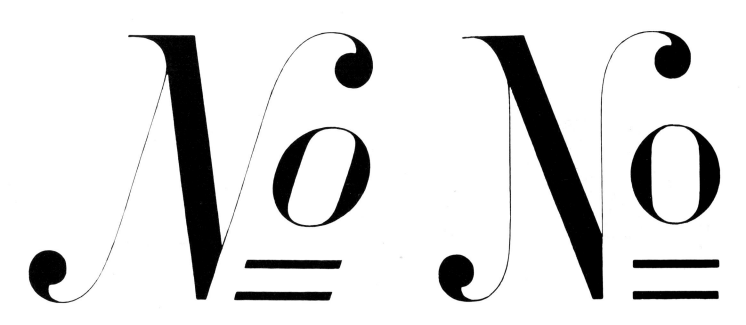

15314 - H

15311 - F

15312 - H

15313 - F

1695 - E

10129 — G

7211 — G

10140 — G

8022 — G

8020 — G

8021 — G

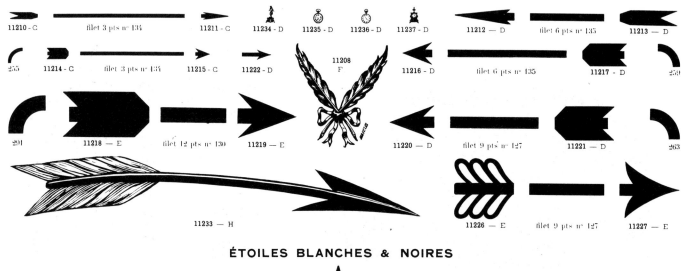

11210 - C   filet 3 pts n° 134   11211 - C   11234 - D   11235 - D   11236 - D   11237 - D   11212 — D   filet 6 pts n° 135   11213 - D

255   11214 - C   filet 3 pts n° 134   11215 - C   11222 - D   11208 F   11216 - D   filet 6 pts n° 135   11217 - D   259

291   11218 — E   filet 12 pts n° 130   11219 — E   11220 - D   filet 9 pts n° 127   11221 — D   263

11233 — H   11226 — E   filet 9 pts n° 127   11227 — E

ÉTOILES BLANCHES & NOIRES

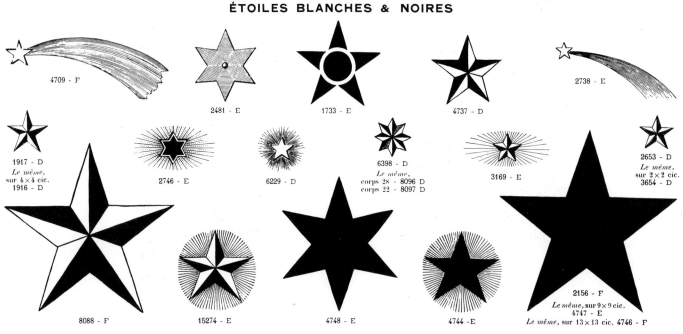

4709 - F

2481 - E

1733 - E

4737 - D

2738 - E

1917 - D
Le même,
sur 4×4 cic.
1916 - D

2746 - E

6229 - D

6398 - D
Le même,
corps 28 - 8096 D
corps 22 - 8097 D

3169 - E

2653 - D
Le même,
sur 2×2 cic.
3654 - D

8088 - F

15274 - E

4748 - E

4744 - E

2156 - F
Le même, sur 9×9 cic.
4747 - E
Le même, sur 13×13 cic. 4746 - F

Voir à la 6° Division du CATALOGUE GÉNÉRAL (page 214), nos ÉTOILES BLANCHES & NOIRES de DIFFÉRENTES DIMENSIONS

RETOUR A LA

NAÏVETÉ

EDITIONS

PAUL MARTIAL

créés et réalisés par

SOYEZ FIER DE VOS BEAUX IMPRIMÉS

Pourquoi cache-t-il le dépliant dans une enveloppe de faire-part ?
Pourquoi cache-t-il son nom à la fin d'un texte rédactionnel ?
Pourquoi être astucieux ? Pourquoi être machiavélique ?
Vous êtes fier de ce que vous fabriquez ! Vous êtes fier de ce que vous vendez !
Annoncez-le dès l'enveloppe.

francis
bernard

912 — F

871 — F

3697 — F

2418 — G

GALVANOS MONTÉS SUR MATIÈRE

La pièce : E

30 On se réunira à la Maison Mortuaire

41 **ON SE RÉUNIRA A LA MAISON MORTUAIRE**

32 *On se réunira à la Maison Mortuaire*

34 On se réunira à la Maison Mortuaire

EN CAS D'OUBLI PRIÈRE D'EN FAIRE PART 42

On se réunira à la Maison Mortuaire 31

Vous êtes prié d'assister aux Convoi, Service et Enterrement de 43

On se réunira à la Maison Mortuaire 33

29 Requiescat in Pace !   44 Un Ange au Ciel !   45 Un Ange au Ciel !   46 Requiescat in Pace !

17 Regrets !

50 Laudate !

18 Pater Noster !

19 De Profundis !

25 Laudate Pueri Dominum !

20 Priez pour Lui !

21 Priez pour Elle !

51 Un Ange au Ciel !

22 Requiescat in Pace !

23 Priez Dieu pour Lui !

24 Priez Dieu pour Elle !

52 De Profundis ! S. V. P.

53 Un De Profundis S. V. P.

54 Priez Dieu pour le repos de son Ame !

LETTRES OMBRÉES

11969 - 56

ABCDEFGHIJ
KLMNOPQR
STUVWX
.,:;YZ-!'
1234567890

40-line.   16-line.

GRO SCARBOROUG

20-line.

ORCHESTR

COIN

ELONGATED SANS No. 324.

40-line   16-line

GR SCARBOR

20-line.

ORCHES

30-line No. 315

GROUND

SEE THIS PUNCH MARK

DELITTLE
YORK

STAMPED ON EVERY "A"

162

SPECIMENS OF WOOD LETTER

MANUFACTURED BY

WRIGHT & CO.,

157, SOUTHWARK BRIDGE ROAD, LONDON, S.E.

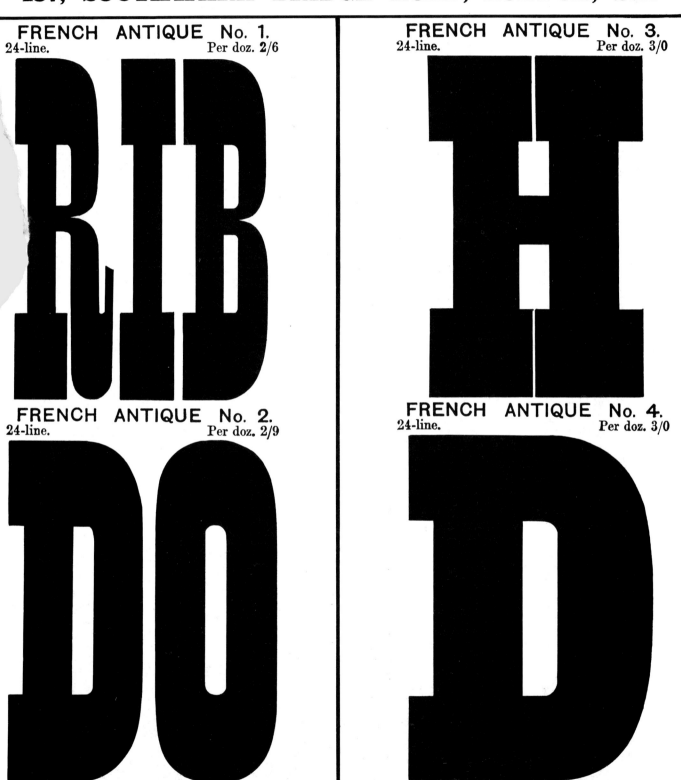

FRENCH ANTIQUE No. 1.
24-line.   Per doz. 2/6

FRENCH ANTIQUE No. 3.
24-line.   Per doz. 3/0

FRENCH ANTIQUE No. 2.
24-line.   Per doz. 2/9

FRENCH ANTIQUE No. 4.
24-line.   Per doz. 3/0

THESE LETTERS CAN BE CUT TO ANY SIZE AT PROPORTIONATE PRICES.

All the above can be supplied cut on Side Grain Box Wood or End Grain Maple at 25% extra.

STUDIO

METROPOLE PUBLICITE

11, Rue de Provence

PARIS

5 rue *Newton*

PARIS-1085N
BD DES ITALIENS

PARIS-1085N
BD DES ITALIENS

SEGUNDO PRÉMIO

VENDIDO PELA FELIZ CASA

TESTA
61585
12.000 CONTOS

NA LOTARIA
DE 27 DE OUTUBRO DE 1989

NÃO ESQUEÇA...
SE QUER FESTA JOGUE NO TESTA

DE HAUKE & Cº

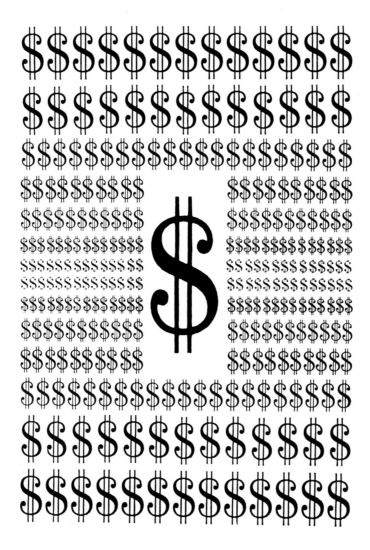

NEW-YORK

ABCDEF
GHIJKL!
MNOPQR
STUVW$
XYZ1234
567890&

ABCDE
FGHIJK
LMNOP
QRSTU
VWXYZ
&$!?&&
12345
67890

ÉDITIONS JEANNE WALTER

26, RUE GEOFFROY-L'ASNIER - PARIS IVᵉ

PARIS

80 PHOTOGRAPHIES

DE MOÏ VER

INTRODUCTION DE

FERNAND LÉGER

ABCDEFG
HIJKLMN
OPQRST!
UVWXYZ
1234567
890&&?

ABCDEFGHIJK
LMNOPQRSTU
VWXYZ0&&&
abcdefghijklmno
pqrstuvwxyz000
1234567890O$

IMAGES DU MONDE

MER
MARINES MARINS

RACES

PAR

PAUL VALÉRY
de l'Académie Française

PAR

JEAN BRUNHES
de l'Institut

Volumes in-quarto écu de 112 pages, illustrés de 96 planches en héliogravure et brochés dans une couverture illustrée en papier fort. Prix : 30 francs. (On souscrit aux 6 premiers volumes de la collection pour 165 francs, payables : 27 fr. 50 à la réception de chaque volume.)

A68

A69

A60

A61

A62

A63

A66

A67

5754 5758 / Corps 4 / Satz ca. 1 kg à M. 15,00
5754 5755 5756 5757 5758

5759 5763 / Corps 6 / Satz ca. 2 kg à M. 9,00
5759 5760 5761 5762 5763

5764 5768 / Corps 9 / Satz ca. 3 kg à M. 8,75
5764 5765 5766 5767 5768

5769 5773 / Corps 12 / Satz ca. 3 kg à M. 8,50
5769 5770 5771 5772 5773

5774 5778 / Corps 18 / Satz ca. 3 kg à M. 8,00
5774 5775 5776 5777 5778

5779 5783 / Corps 24 / Satz ca. 4 kg à M. 7,50
5779 5780 5781 5782 5783

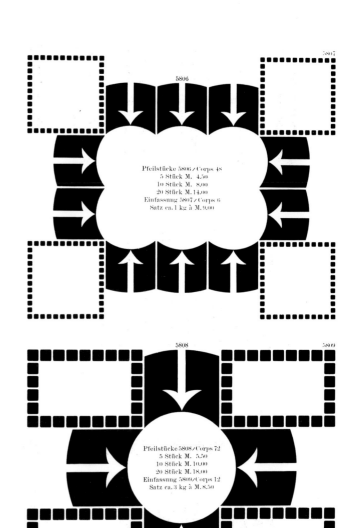

5806
5807

Pfeilstücke 5806 / Corps 48
5 Stück M. 4,50
10 Stück M. 8,00
20 Stück M. 14,00
Einfassung 5807 / Corps 6
Satz ca. 1 kg à M. 9,00

5808
5809

Pfeilstücke 5808 / Corps 72
5 Stück M. 5,50
10 Stück M. 10,00
20 Stück M. 18,00
Einfassung 5809 / Corps 12
Satz ca. 3 kg à M. 8,50

ABCDEFGHIJKLMN

OPQRSTUVWXYZ&

abcdefghijklmnopqrstuvwxyz

ABCDFGHIJ
KLMNOPQR
STUVWXYZ
OPERN~MUSIK

MANUFACTURED BY MACKELLAR, SMITHS & JORDAN FOUNDRY, PHILADELPHIA

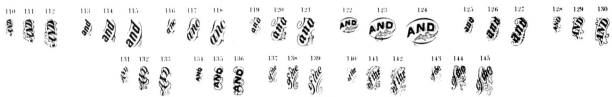

110 111 112   113 114 115   116 117 118   119 120 121   122   123   124   125 126 127   128 129 130

131 132 133   134 135 136   137 138 139   140 141 142   143 144 145

PRICE, PER FONT, $3.00

 No. 93. 35 cts.
 No. 92. 30 cts.
 No. 95. 40 cts.
 No. 94. 40 cts.
 No. 96. 40 cts.

 No. 101. 40 cts.
 No. 99. 35 cts.
 No. 97. 40 cts.
 No. 104. 40 cts.
 No. 98. 35 cts.

 No. 102. 40 cts.
 No. 100. 40 cts.
 No. 106. 40 cts.
 No. 103. 40 cts.

 No. 107. 40 cts.
 No. 108. 40 cts.
 No. 105. 40 cts.
 No. 109. 40 cts.

PRICE, PER FONT, $5.00

 No. 332. 75 cts.
 No. 3951. 75 cts.
 No. 91. 75 cts.

 No. 310. 45 cts.
 No. 333. 75 cts.
 No. 3950. 75 cts.

 No. 90. 75 cts.
 No. 331. 75 cts.
 No. 307. 40 cts.

No. 4066. 75 cts.

No. 4059. 75 cts.

No. 4058. 75 cts.

No. 4073. 50 cts.

No. 4062. 75 cts.

No. 4075. 50 cts.

No. 4070. 60 cts.

No. 4067. 60 cts.

No. 4055. 50 cts.

No. 4061. 50 cts.

No. 4071. 75 cts.

No. 4063. 60 cts.

No. 4072. 75 cts.

No. 4060. 60 cts.

No. 4068. 75 cts.

No. 4069. 75 cts.

No. 4056. 75 cts.

No. 4065. 75 cts.

No. 4054. 75 cts.

No. 4064. 75 cts.

No. 4074. 75 cts.

No. 4057. 75 cts.

ELECTRIC ORNAMENTS

ORIGINATED BY AMERICAN TYPE FOUNDERS' CO., NEW YORK

COMPLETE FONT $2 50

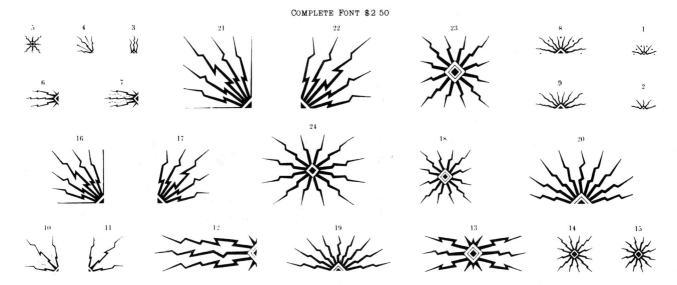

The font contains 140 pieces. 1 and 2, twelve each; 3, eight; 4, 6, 7, 8, 9, 10, 11, 16, 17, 18, 21, 22, 23, four each;
5, thirty-six [six inches]; 12, 13, 19, 20, 24, two each; 14, 15, five each

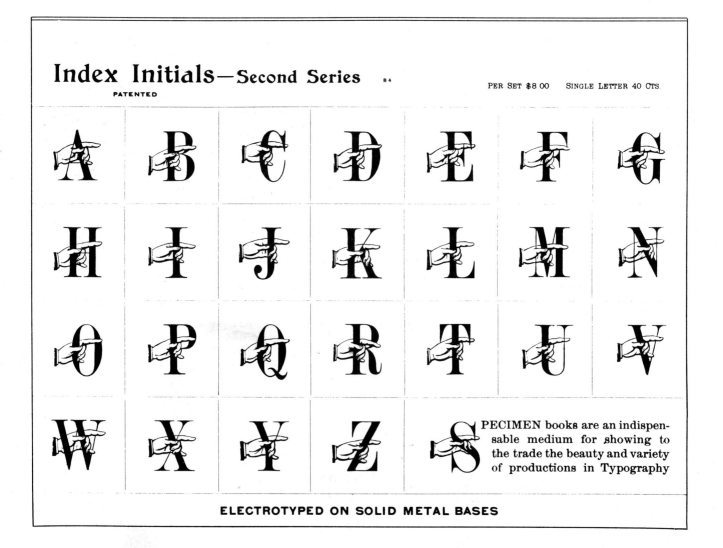

Index Initials—Second Series

PATENTED

PER SET $8.00   SINGLE LETTER 40 CTS.

SPECIMEN books are an indispensable medium for showing to the trade the beauty and variety of productions in Typography

ELECTROTYPED ON SOLID METAL BASES

VIEUX
MOULINS A PAPIER
D'AUVERGNE
(Suite du n° 53.)

COMMENT TRAVAILLENT
LES PAPETIERS D'AUVERGNE

De pur chiffon. Telle semble la devise de leurs produits. Concurrencés par les usines plus modernes de l'Ardèche et de l'Isère, le papier d'édition est à peu près disparu de l'Auvergne. Quelques rares amateurs ou éditeurs y ont encore recours de temps à autre. Mais, c'est là, plus une curiosité bibliophilique qu'une production courante.

Par contre, le papier filtre et le papier Joseph (papier très fin pour la pharmacie et les laboratoires) y sont encore réalisés dans trois moulins : un à Toulouse (atelier Chantelauze) et deux à Lagat (Favier père et fils et Jean Lebon).

A la Forie, la fabrication est devenue mécanique et le moulin de Lebon-Bonnefoy réalise du papier buvard de pur chiffon.

Enfin le papier gris foncé dit *laineux*, utilisé pour garnir les cylindres de calandres à papier, occupe un moulin à la Forie et deux autres à Lagat.

Nous laisserons de côté *buvard* et *laineux*, à technique nettement mécanique, pour n'examiner que la fabrication réellement manuelle des papiers filtre et Joseph.

La matière première. — Les chiffons ou *drapeaux*, comme on les appelait autrefois, n'ont plus, actuellement, à venir de fort loin, de la vallée de la Saône ou du Rhône et subir ainsi moult péages et droits de circulation provinciaux et citadins.

Diamond Combination Monograms

Sold in sets containing the 78 characters shown or in monograms containing any three characters

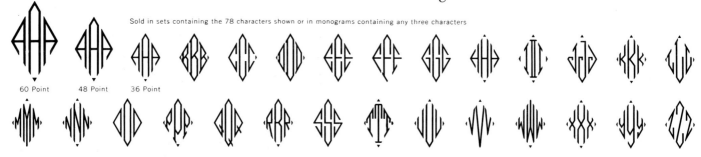

60 Point   48 Point   36 Point

Elite Monograms

Font contains 3 of each of the characters shown except Mc. Sold in fonts, or in 3-letter monograms containing initials of different sizes if desired.

60 Point 48 Point 36 Point

Broadway Monograms

Fonts contain one each of the larger letters A to Z and two each of the small letters. The larger letters are cast recessed at top and bottom to permit the insertion of the small characters without any justification. Sold in complete fonts containing one each of the 78 characters shown, or in monograms containing any three characters.

Fifth Avenue Monograms and Frames

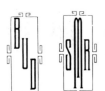

Fonts of initials contain three of each letter cast on 54 point body, and three of each letter cast on 24 point body. The M and W are 8 points wide; all other characters are 6 points wide. Sold in fonts containing 156 characters, or in monograms containing any three characters.

Frames are cast on 72 point body in two mortised pieces. The seven widths accommodate any two- or three-letter combination. Sold by the single pair, or in sets containing one pair of each of the 7 styles shown at right.

Combinations consisting of any 3-letter monogram and a single pair of frames may also be ordered.

 No. 1 — 12 Point mortise

 No. 2 — 14 Point mortise

No. 3 — 16 Point mortise

No. 4 — 18 Point mortise

No. 5 — 20 Point mortise

No. 6 — 22 Point mortise

No. 7 — 24 Point mortise

Newport Monograms

Sold in fonts containing three each of the one-color or tint characters shown, or in monograms containing any 3 characters.

Cast on 36 point body, 12 point set, except the I (9 point) and M and W (18 point). All cast to register for two color printing.

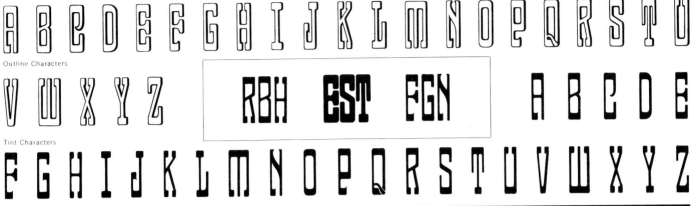

Outline Characters

Tint Characters

Virkotype Combination Monograms

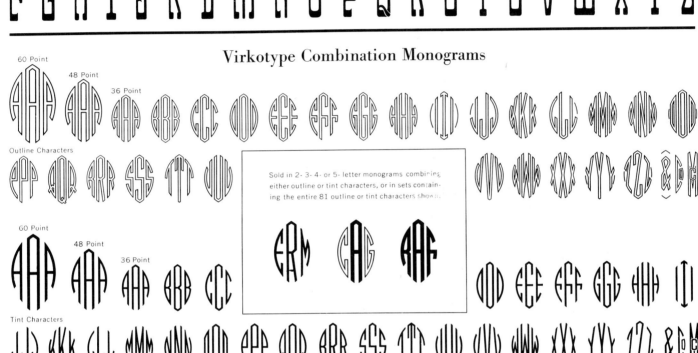

Outline Characters

Sold in 2- 3- 4- or 5- letter monograms combining either outline or tint characters, or in sets containing the entire 81 outline or tint characters shown.

Tint Characters

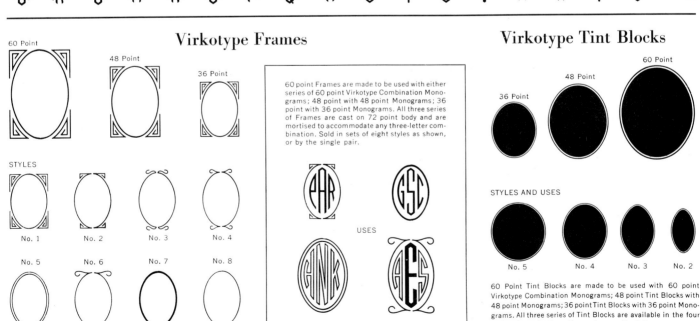

Virkotype Frames

60 Point   48 Point   36 Point

60 point Frames are made to be used with either series of 60 point Virkotype Combination Monograms; 48 point with 48 point Monograms; 36 point with 36 point Monograms. All three series of Frames are cast on 72 point body and are mortised to accommodate any three-letter combination. Sold in sets of eight styles as shown, or by the single pair.

USES

STYLES

No. 1   No. 2   No. 3   No. 4

No. 5   No. 6   No. 7   No. 8

Virkotype Tint Blocks

60 Point

48 Point

36 Point

STYLES AND USES

No. 5   No. 4   No. 3   No. 2

60 Point Tint Blocks are made to be used with 60 point Virkotype Combination Monograms; 48 point Tint Blocks with 48 point Monograms; 36 point Tint Blocks with 36 point Monograms. All three series of Tint Blocks are available in the four styles shown for two-, three-, four-,or five-letter monograms.

13250
13249
13251
13216
13223

13239
13221
13240
13237
13236
13217
13224
13225

13230
13226
13229
13241
13242

13234
13235
13243
13233
13244

13231
13232
13213
13301
13302
13214

13222
13218
13219
13247
13220
13248

13238
13252

13253

13227
13228
13254

FINISHED.

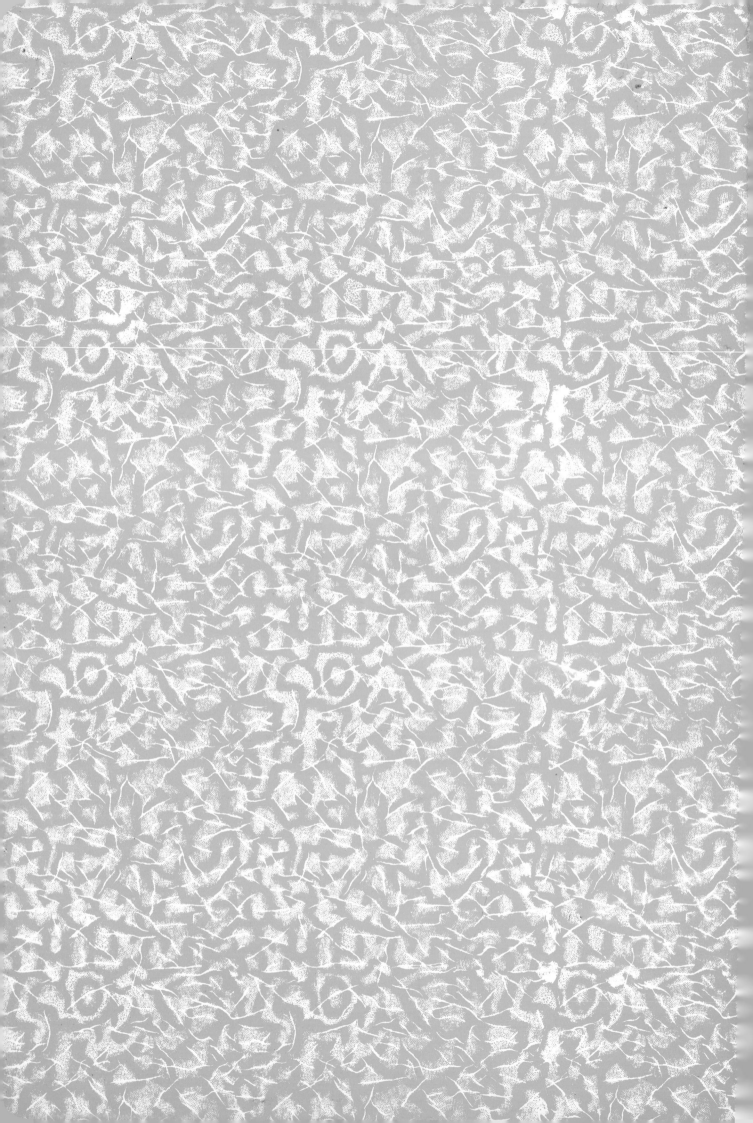